FRIENDS OF ACPL

3 1833 05560 3406

D0932860

OCT 1 4 2010

Allah's Garden:

A True Story of a Forgotten War in the Sahara Desert of Morocco

The agony of Azeddine, a Moroccan prisoner of war in the camps run by Polisario, is a sad reminder of the cost of war in Western Sahara paid by men, women and children far removed from the centers of power in Rabat, Algiers, Washington DC and European capitals. Although Morocco enjoys a stable reputation in the West, the unresolved Western Sahara dispute calls for rapid intervention if not on political or ideological grounds, then on humanitarian. Thomas Hollowell's powerful narrative illustrates this urgency, and it is an excellent account of a humanitarian disaster that started more than 35 years ago.

- James N. Sater, author of *Morocco: Challenges to Tradition and Modernity* (New York: Routledge, 2009).

Other Books by Tales Press

Iwo Blasted Again
by Ray Elliott

Wild Hands Towards the Sky
by Ray Elliott

Pin A Medal On Me
by Geil Evans Butler

Bittersweet: The Story of the Heath Candy Co.
by Richard J. Heath with Ray Elliott

Good Morning – But the Nightmares Never End
by Charlie Dukes

We Can All Get Along If…
Tales Press Cultural Journalism Project

Born in Illinois Cornfields
by Alvin Decker

Bait
by Donald E. Stephen

Writings from the Handy Colony
Edited by Helen Howe, Don Sackrider, & George Hendrick

For more information about Tales Press books,
visit vwww.TalesPress.com

Allah's Garden:

A True Story of a Forgotten War in the Sahara Desert of Morocco

Thomas Hollowell

Tales Press
Urbana, Illinois USA

Copyright © 2009 by Thomas Hollowell
All rights reserved. Published 2009.
Address inquiries to Tales Press, 2609 North High Cross Road
Urbana, IL 61802 USA
Visit our Web site at www.TalesPress.com

First Edition, 2009 by Tales Press, Urbana, Illinois USA

Library of Congress Cataloging-in-Publication Data

Hollowell, Thomas, 1978-
  Allah's garden / Thomas Hollowell. -- 1st ed.
     p. cm.
  ISBN-13: 978-0-9641423-9-8 (pbk. : alk. paper)
  ISBN-10: 0-9641423-9-2 (pbk. : alk. paper)
1. Morocco--Description and travel. 2. Peace Corps (U.S.)--
Morocco. 3. Hostages--Morocco. I. Title.
  DT310.3.H65 2009
  964.05'3--dc22
                              2008047288

No part of this publication may be reproduced, stored in a retriev-
al system, or transmitted in any form or by any means, without the
prior written consent of the copyright holder. This book does not
intend to misrepresent any person, group, ethnicity, or organization. The publisher accepts no liability or responsibility as a result
of the information contained herein.

Edited By: Ariele Huff
Typeset and Morocco Map By: Susan Reed
Cover Design: Adina Cucicov, Flamingo Designs
Consultation: Sherice Jacob at iElectrify.com
Cover Photos: © iStockphoto/Mlenny

Printed in the United States of America and elsewhere abroad.

Author's Note

This narrative took me much farther into Morocco than I'd agreed upon when I joined the volunteer organization called the Peace Corps. It took me all over Morocco, through its culture, language, history, and deep into the Saharan sands. I have learned that this desert will never yield itself. It's simply too vast, too intricate, and too deep.

All of the happenings in this tale are based on true events. Writing the book in narrative form and using Azeddine's plight as the backdrop opened up the flexibility and essential literary tools needed to bring this recounting to life. A few characters presented are fictive personages personifying and embodying a collective group, theme, or event. Creative inferences were used to shape characters, portray events, and frame conversations. The story is based on months of taped interviews with the protagonist, my time with and without the Peace Corps in Morocco, and various political, social, and individual occurrences. Research was also conducted through on-the-ground fieldwork and the reading of various articles, exposés, newspapers, and other books, such as the superbly documented prisoner's memoir *L'Horreur* by Moroccan author Abdellah Lamani. Certain scenes are inspired by and indebted to these portrayals.

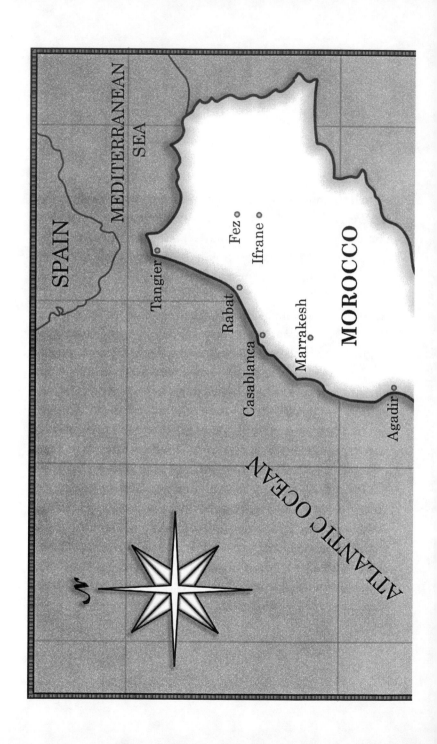

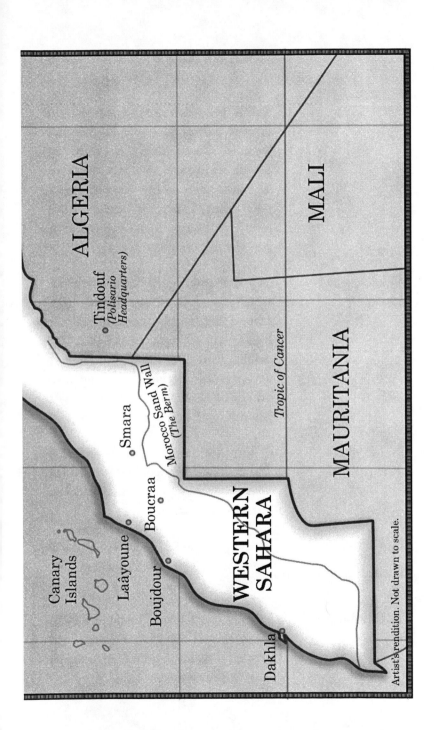

ALGERIA

MALI

Tindouf
(Polisario Headquarters)

Tropic of Cancer

MAURITANIA

Smara

Morocco Sand Wall
(The Berm)

Boucraa

WESTERN SAHARA

Laâyoune

Boujdour

Canary
Islands

Dakhla

Artist's rendition. Not drawn to scale.

Timeline of Events
Related to Western Sahara:

1884-1975
Spain colonizes and controls the Spanish Sahara (modern-day Western Sahara). They divide it into the Saquia el-Hamra and Rio de Oro. The Saharawis of the interior region rebel often. Later, the land is found rich in minerals, including oil, iron, manganese, and phosphate.

October 1963
Morocco and Algeria battle in a three-week war dubbed the "Sand War" around the Tindouf (current Polisario Headquarters) area of Algeria. The conflict arose due to ambiguous French demarcations, previously calling areas of the Sahara uninhabitable with "superfluous" borders.

10 May 1973
Official formation of the Polisario. The organization's goal was to rid the Spanish Sahara (Western Sahara) of Spanish occupation.

20 May 1973
El Khanga Attack: The Polisario makes its first armed guerilla raid against the Spanish occupiers.

16 October 1975
International Court of Justice rules that Morocco and Mauritania do not have a right to claim territorial sovereignty over Western Sahara.

3 1833 05569 3490

January 1975	Spain prepares itself to depart the Spanish Sahara, leaving the land now fully titled the "Western Sahara" to its fate.
6-9 November 1975	Green March takes place. Moroccan citizens peacefully enter Western Sahara.
14 November 1975	The Madrid Accords treaty is signed between Spain, Morocco, and Mauritania to fully end Spain's occupation of Western Sahara. Morocco is entitled to the northern two-thirds, while Mauritania keeps with the bottom one-third. Spain is allowed to keep certain profits of the Bu Craa phosphate enterprise.
27 February 1976	Declaration and formation of the Saharawi Arab Democratic Republic (SADR).
February 1976	The massive Battle of Amgala, an oasis in Western Sahara, takes place and is the first time Algerian Forces directly back the Polisario against Morocco's Royal Armed Forces (FAR). Amgala becomes the scene for future skirmishes.
24 August 1979	Polisario attack Lebouirate, where the young Dr. Azeddine Benmansour is captured. Progressing, the Polisario fight into Smara and take over Mahbes, among other key locations.

8 August 1979	Mauritania drops claims to Western Sahara.
1980-1987	Construction on the Moroccan Sand Wall (Berm) takes place. By its completion, it is 1,678 miles (2,700 km) in length, about half the size of the Great Wall of China.
Early 1984	The Red Cross (Croix Rouge) is allowed to enter the camps to attend to a limited number of prisoners. The Polisario subsequently release ten prisoners.
25 May 1987	One hundred and fifty Moroccan POWs in Polisario camps are exchanged for 102 Algerian POWs held by Morocco from the battle of Amgala.
November 1989	The Polisario releases 200 prisoners who wait another six years for their repatriation back into Morocco; King Hassan II insisted on all Moroccan POWs being released at the same time. Several of these in waiting passed away.
26 August 1991	The last major battle between the Royal Armed Forces (FAR) and the Polisario occurs.
6 September 1991	Ceasefire declared over Western Sahara. The UN's MINURSO oversees delegations with offices set

up in Layounne. The result is a political stalemate that continues today.

December 1991	Algerian Civil War begins. This results in less focus on and funding of the Polisario from Algeria.
23 July 1999	Hassan II passes away. His son and heir, Mohammed VI, becomes king. He improves diplomatic ties and relations within the kingdom, and with Algeria and the world.
1 September 2003	Azeddine and others are released and flown to Agadir, Morocco. Certain groups are freed before this. Following their liberation, POWs are reunited with their respective families.

to Azeddine and pure human courage

Contents

Part One: Echoes of Death

As outlined by the World Health Organization, all prisoners we have seen are suffering physical and/or emotional maladies. For this reason, all need to be immediately treated.... The actual health conditions of the prisoners cannot be fully analyzed as many of the population have been in the camps of upwards near twenty-five years.... The systematic emotional and physical abuse over these many years has affected everyone and cannot be calculated on any understood scale. The forced labor and abuse without protection, plus the increased risk of injury due to work has left many prisoners handicapped or dead.... All the conditions here give any doctor visiting under the International Red Cross an impression that this place is a concentration camp. These prisoners, nonetheless, are suffering against everything outlined in the Geneva Conventions [1949].... The prisoners eat neither fruits nor vegetables. Outside aid has helped the situation some. Our visits were done with the help and precious time and information provided by Doctor [Azeddine] Benmansour (EHT 00612) and four other nurses.

- Confidentially obtained medical records from the International Red Cross (IRC): Medical report of Moroccans detained by the Polisario Front. April 2000 in Tindouf, Algeria & IRC Internal Medical Report: 12/10/1998 to Florence Sechaud, IRC Tunisia.

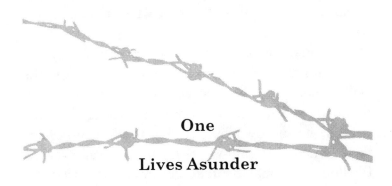

One

Lives Asunder

24 August 1979 Sahara Desert, Morocco

"...Mohammed Rasulullah!" Azeddine chanted as the eastern hills reverberated the bombs blasting the crumbling kasbah walls. The sky ignited the horizon with shades of pink and tinges of orange, casting an amber hue over the distant sand dunes and the closer, rock-strewn terrain. "Allah Akbar. Estaghfer Allah!" The death mantra crept uncontrollably to his lips, replacing the morning's usual salat prayer.

An explosive sound shook the walls. The metal plates inside the windows clanked against the bars. Sand, dirt, and rubble blew underneath the door, which sat unevenly on rusted hinges. Azeddine bit down on his tongue. Sand continued to wisp inward.

As he ran toward the wooden doors of the infirmary, Azeddine heard Ahmed scream. Rushing in, he bent over, breathless. The Moroccan fountain in the middle of the waiting area wasn't flowing. No soldiers had arrived yet. Most were a part of the enfilade that was to barricade the town—to secure where the outer wall had failed.

Two nurses, however, worked hastily under one lit bulb that reflected off the pasty blue walls back in the "salle d'hospitalisation," located on the other side of the corridor. The place was normally organized despite being a bit run-down, but now it was a disaster. Chairs were turned over and papers lay scattered all over the tile floor. The small dental office door was closed. No nurses were in the triage room or in the nurses' station.

Azeddine quickly headed to the back ward, still catching his breath. Working to unpack gauze and roll the beds in a straight line against the back wall, he didn't feel like a professional doctor, but an ill-prepared pupil who was facing fate head-on.

Dr. Ahmed and Head Nurse Omar burst through the door. Ahmed was saying something in a mix of Arabic and French about getting the place secure. "Put the defense covers over the windows!" Ahmed had survived an attack some two weeks prior, which was all Azeddine knew. Ahmed's eyes still had dark circles beneath them and he squinted as if he were forcing his eyes open to face the world. Since so much was left unsaid, Azeddine never overcame his uneasiness when he was around the sturdy man. He only knew that Ahmed had been in this small, dusty village when the attack occurred, somewhere on the edge of what felt like the end of the world.

The doors flew open, and two soldiers carried in an injured Moroccan cadet.

The young trainee bellowed uncontrollably,

"ALLAH!" His right leg looked like it had been torn off at the knee. Embedded with layers of ground-up skin, it was ripped apart. Bright blood spurted out onto the floor.

As if he'd been planning for this day repeatedly in his mind, Ahmed knew exactly what to do. Was it the bloodshed he'd already lived through? Was he ready this time to go down fighting?

The two soldiers ran out as soon as they laid their injured comrade on a gurney.

Azeddine could see them from the pharmacy room. The soldier's leg had been horribly severed. Nurse Omar grabbed a tourniquet and wrapped it tightly around the bleeding stump. He removed the upper pant and tried to soak up the blood with a sponge, then grabbed a dirty towel.

Two more Moroccan men—one dressed in a captain's uniform, the other a chauffeur's—rushed in. The driver slammed the door behind them as they approached.

Azeddine swallowed hard and forced himself to walk away from his patients toward them. His eyes dropped to the captain's right arm. It dangled unnaturally from the elbow. He knew it was broken, although no bones were exposed.

Ahmed was busy with the cadet. Azeddine wasn't quite sure how to handle the situation. He wanted to look at the captain's arm but couldn't ask him to remove his shirt. The officer was a higher rank and much older; even in an emergency, he'd have to adhere to societal norms. Instead, he asked the captain to remove his jacket, and then slowly tore off the sleeve.

He was trying to hold back his shaking hands as he put the captain's arm in a sling, but he still heard the piercing wails of the young soldier behind him.

The captain looked as if he were trying to examine the old infirmary, then he turned, looked up at Azeddine, and asserted quietly yet sternly that he was leaving. He told Azeddine and the rest they should do the same. The withdrawal route had already been prepared, and they would die if they didn't admit defeat.

"Retreat. Live!" is all that Azeddine heard as the captain headed out.

Azeddine looked over at the injured soldier, then back to the retreating captain. Azeddine followed the commander to the infirmary doors, trying to keep his voice down as he explained about all the patients flooding in, how there was nowhere else for them to go, and how they couldn't simply abandon them there.

The captain pointed at the gurneys. "Luck will only take you so far!" he told Azeddine in Moroccan Arabic, known as Darija. The captain's cheeks drooped and looked heavily flushed. His throaty voice emitted a "Layownkoom." God help you.

Ambulances arrived bringing in more injured soldiers and civilians. Men with shrapnel and bullet wounds lay in agony. One had a swollen eye. The encrusted blood looked like a dried-up waterfall caked on his cheek. Azeddine had nothing to clean it with.

A morphine drip and a bag of blood trickled into the soldier missing his leg. The rough tourniquet held back the dam of blood, but like a leaky faucet, small droplets still dripped onto the floor. The tinge of blue on the soldier's hand indicated it might be too late; he'd already lost so much blood. Azeddine raised his eyes up to the soldier's. A jolt shot through Azeddine as he remembered this smiling, young soldier playing ball with a Berber boy outside the infirmary just days ago. The soldier lying in front of him wasn't even a man yet. Maybe he would never be. It couldn't be his time.

On the next gurney lay a soldier who'd been shot in the shoulder. The wound was high enough that nothing vital was damaged. His eyes were closed. He wheezed in and out. Azeddine whispered a prayer and pulled the sheet up to the man's chest as he looked at the wound, preparing for the quick removal of the shrapnel.

The beds were filled. The captain had fled. Why couldn't Azeddine and the others do the same? He watched as many struggled to breathe. Ahmed looked from across the room as if trying to say something, but was at a loss for words.

Many of the patients were still alive. "Allah, shnoo radi ndirou?" Azeddine mumbled. Allah, what are we going to do? He sat for a moment. It was all he could do to keep himself together. He didn't have his prayer beads, a gift from his mother to remember Allah's 99 sacred titles. Ahmed looked up again at Azeddine. Only when Azeddine looked down at his open, shaking hands did he truly realize his own limitations. There would be no miracles.

Two

Cultural Mayhem

1999 to spring 2002

TWO MOROCCAN students at Wabash College in Indiana, a university of 800 men, talked one evening at dinner to me and my identical twin brother, Terry, about the people and Mediterranean vista near Tangier, Morocco. They told us stories about endless summers on pristine beaches, the eerie blue water where the Atlantic and Mediterranean meet, and the Cave of Hercules. Over the span of a week, we met a few times over dinner, discussing their home country.

The famed artist, Henri Matisse, had frequented Tangier with religious regularity searching for the inspiring colors described by Delacroix. The city had a growing eccentric appeal, especially by the time Paul Bowles and William S. Burroughs set foot on its sandy terrain. This northern city, just a stone's throw south of Spain, had become an international zone—a new epicenter of European and American debauchery. Tangier became a new figurative and literary playground. It was an *Interzone* full of opportunity for expression and indulgence.

In their dorm room, the Moroccan students had a replica of an ancient, cream-colored travel poster of Tangier. The center of the scene merged to the forefront where a man of genteel heritage sipped a cup of tea. In the background, the walled city spread out into the horizon; mosques towered over the square houses. The poster invited all from far and wide to experience the newfound sovereignty.

Tangier prospered in the 1920s and 1930s. Common was the smuggling of drugs and contraband. International spy networks used Tangier as a haven, if not as a place to convene. The rich used it for offshore banking. Once World War II hit, Spain decided to watch over the newly formed conurbation, perhaps hoping that one day they could contend the territory. Morocco, however, reclaimed the territory in the mid-1950s. The city lost much of what gave it a daring, secretive, avant-garde zest.

My brother discovered a tattered *Lonely Planet Morocco* guidebook in the International Studies building on campus. He confirmed that Morocco was geographically similar to California. It had mountains and thousands of miles of coastline, not to mention a sizable chunk of desert.

On a foldout map displaying Morocco in its entirety, a small dotted line separated the upper half of Morocco from what appeared to be its lower half. After some supplementary research, we learned that under this dotted line, this perplexing underbelly of Morocco was once called the Spanish Sahara.

Labeled now as Western Sahara, an expansive history of the region was left untold. Little did I realize, as I do now, how its sands engulfed like quicksand those who trod daringly close.

Coincidentally, as Terry and I were researching this North African country, a Travel Channel special dedicated to Morocco aired. One line in the entire thirty-minute special described it best in saying that the Maghreb, the land of the setting sun, had a brilliant radiance that could only be illustrated as tangerine-orange.

According to the show, the beaches along Morocco's Atlantic coast were superb, while the strangest, most magical beach was Essaouira. The tangerine-orange and the beaches of Essaouira, known in Arabic as "Sweara" (or picture) in reference to its alluring vistas, filled our minds with wanderlust for quite some time.

After college, Terry and I set off to Costa Rica for our very first adventure abroad. After securing a "paid" volunteer stint—where we paid an organization to volunteer—we left for three months, living in the mountains and getting in the way of park rangers in Chirripó National Park. We lived with host families, practiced Spanish, skinny dipped with travelers in the town's famed hot spring, and wagered which of our nine host sisters would get pregnant, again.

Upon our return to the USA, I started reading more about North Africa, which heightened my desire to visit Morocco. Until I could get there, I began teaching at a center for at-risk youth. Terry started work on his Master's Degree.

To friends and family back home, Morocco might as well be the capital of Antarctica. Hoosiers, as Indiana locals are referred to, are proud to be the world's leading popcorn producer and are a warm-hearted bunch. But many regions lean to the conservative and are not overly adept with the gift of geographical gab. With many residents, mentioning a far-flung locale gets you a side-ways, doggish glance.

In Indianapolis, I met with a well-groomed representative from the Peace Corps who was holding a meeting with potential volunteers. In a white shirt, blue tie, and a nametag written with marker that read "Jeremy," the recruiter asked me several questions. "What would you miss if you left the country for two years? Do you have any health concerns?" And finally, "If you are involved in a relationship, how would you and your partner handle the separation?"

I wasn't sure how to answer some of the questions, but I attempted to do so as smoothly as possible. I had never left the country for that long before, so how would I know? I had had some knee problems in the past. And, I had been involved in a serious relationship that was on the brink of implosion. *How to answer? How not to set off any red flags?*

Excited at the possibilities, I'd perhaps have an opportunity to explore the mysteries of Africa. The sign-up form indicated to circle which region of the world I would be interested in serving. While South America, Africa, or the Pacific Islands were options, I didn't circle anything, but wrote quickly what looked like MARCO. The representative asked me who "Marco" was.

"Morocco," I clarified.

"We can't guarantee anything. If you are invited somewhere else, it is because you match a need elsewhere."

"What if I don't accept an invitation to serve in another country?"

"That would be looked down upon—if you don't have a valid excuse."

The application process was a game of patience and perseverance. While awaiting a response, I began reading more about the Peace Corps. A book entitled *So, You Want to Join the Peace Corps* laid down the realities of the organization. It also talked about the practicalities of living abroad. How will I learn the language? What should I expect from the Peace Corps organization itself? Should I have a maid? *A maid!*

Plus, I had more tasks to complete for Washington D.C., a Big-Brother entity who carefully assessed who was fit for what type of service. Included in the process, I was to turn in all past medical records and have a dental checkup.

The dental examination involved a machine that circumnavigated my jaw, shooting a constant ray of radiation through my skull. As the dentist stood behind his protective lead panel, he assured me that an hour of direct exposure to the sun gave a greater concentration than this machine. He mentioned afterwards that I should not have an x-ray for another three months. The incongruity of this fact with his earlier nonchalant statement didn't add up. It didn't matter. I knew it would all be worth it. Following the exam, the dentist said I would have to have my four wisdom teeth pulled out. I thought to myself: *This better be worth it.*

Dental surgery came the following week. Surgery left my face bloated up like a small woodland creature, cheeks stuffed and puffed, preparing for winter. All that was left of my mouth was a small slit from which I could slurp milkshakes, applesauce, and pureed food abhorred by babies and nursing home tenants the world over.

The fear of scaring the neighborhood kids kept me indoors. Using my tongue to properly pronounce the consonants, I looked in the mirror and said out loud with a slight lisp, "It better be worth it."

Months later as the fall leaves fell to the ground, a postal delivery truck dropped off a thick Fed-Ex envelope. My brother stood beside me as I sat down on the stairs and ripped open the envelope. Pulling out the first piece of paper, the insignia at the top revealed a document from the Peace Corps.

"Funny the government doesn't use the USPS."

"Read the letter!" Terry urged.

My heart raced as my eyes zigzagged across the page until I reached the bottom: "…invited to serve in Morocco with the Peace Corps," was all I needed to read. I was elated. Terry was thrilled, but slightly forlorn.

"What do I do now?"

"Run inside and tell Mom!"

Peace Corps Training (called PCT—as government agencies are wont to do by applying their *official* acronyms) came and went in a flash. Terry and I gripped each other as I tossed my daypack onto the airport security machine's x-ray belt. My mother had tears in her eyes. Peering back at their stares and half-waves, I walked to the flight that would take me to Philadelphia, followed by a bus trip to New York City, and a direct flight to Morocco.

After crossing the Atlantic in the longest flight I'd until then been on, we arrived in a metropolitan city of Morocco recognizable to most Americans because of Humphrey Bogart's romantic portrayal in the early 1940s film of the same name, *Casablanca*.

A portly, smiling Peace Corps representative gave us brown bags filled with fruit and nuts. As we rode along together in white mini-vans, I saw rickety houses with tin roofs, black plastic bags waving in the breeze, and decrepit and uncovered wells lining the highway.

After ten days of receiving vaccinations, practicing newly learned Arabic phrases, and living with host families in the colonial-looking capital city of Rabat, we headed south to Ouarzazate, where we would have language training for three months. Darija and Berber with a dash of French became our focus. Mud rooms. Homestays. Meat stews, called tagines. Bread. Olive oil. Volunteers in West Africa were jealous that those serving in Morocco had so many amenities. We were dubbed the "Posh Corps."

During training, loneliness was the common denominator amongst volunteers. I wasn't able to call home often; however, I kept busy by flirting with one of the Peace Corps' official Moroccan language instructors named Sanae, an intriguing girl with captivating eyes.

We knew and agreed that we'd only be able to show

our affections once my training had ended. To do so before becoming an official volunteer would mean my removal from the program. On the last day of training, I stood before the governor of Ouarzazate and the Ambassador to the United States in Morocco with my hand raised and, thereafter, became a full-fledged volunteer of the United States Peace Corps. It was a two-year commitment to this governmental organization established by John F. Kennedy in 1961, whose goals were laid out and still continue to this day: to help those in resource-poor nations, promote world peace, and exchange cultural understanding with people of developing nations.

The next morning, I hopped on a bus to Marrakesh. I longed for some freedom after three months of intensive training and extended homestays with village families.

At the Menara Gardens, a square pool of murky green water, two kilometers away from the famous Djema el Fna Square, I met Sanae. We sat next to the pavilion where, if not for the continual smoggy haze of the city, we'd have a clear view of the High Atlas Mountains in the background. We kissed each other lightly. The area attracted locals and tourists who wanted to enjoy the cool environs while strolling around the surrounding orchards and olive groves.

"Is this your wife?" two Moroccan men asked me in English as they approached closely.

"Why does it matter to you? Seer!" Go away!

"They are patrolmen," Sanae said to me as she let go of my arm. "They are holding to Islamic Law."

"You both. Come with us."

"You've got to be joking!"

"You are fraternizing," one with a nice leather jacket said nonchalantly. "This is illegal."

They believed Sanae to be one of Marrakesh's numerous "entertainment specialists." They escorted us to a Renault van with a faded red insignia reading "Sécurité National." Rusty wire grates over the windows, along with cracked top-mounted red and green lights meant that government funding didn't filter down to the civil forces. These undercover police did everything to convince us (save physical force) to get into the back of the van.

"We are going to check your hymen!" they ranted in Arabic to Sanae once they slammed the van doors shut. They said that it was their duty to ensure she was still a virgin. "All we need is a medical certificate."

In desperation, Sanae said, "Give them money. They will take it!"

I offered them the equivalent of 80 dollars to let us out of the van, probably more than half a month's salary.

"Put your money away! Do you want more trouble?"

They drove to a health center, still threatening to check her virginity.

"Check mine too. I'm a virgin too! Take us back to the center of town. You are not serious!" I was desperate and furious.

At the medical facility, we didn't go inside, but stayed in the parking area. Sanae and I sat and stared at each other, as if we were playing a game of who could stare the longest. Our sudden disinterest got the driver even more heated.

"We want the truth," the driver said in English. We didn't say anything and simply sat in the back of the van. The driver shrugged and started the van, as if he wanted to prove his power over us even more.

At a decrepit police station with empty, yellow walls somewhere far from the center of Marrakesh, we sat for hours on a bench behind bars that one might picture in an old John Wayne movie. We signed some sort of papers that, according to the officers, would mean we could leave.

"There will be more to sign," said the plain-clothes cop.

The documents were written in Fus'ha, classical Arabic. By this point, our minds were fried; our eyes followed to the click-click of the typewriter from where we sat.

That same day, the police shipped us into court. In front of three judges, each wearing a black gown and perched high above on a fortified stage, Sanae and I were not allowed to talk.

Guilty, the judge motioned. We didn't even get to speak in the five-minute hearing. "Return in three weeks … final sentencing."

We were released without a real feeling of freedom. In a manic state of despair, I called the Peace Corps Director from the rooftop of the cheap hotel where I was staying. Next, she called the American ambassador—the one I stood before in Ouarzazate. The ambassador's office called this or that office.

In the middle of all of this, it was recommended that I return to Rabat to clarify everything that had happened. During my time there, I was introduced to a psychologist from Austria. He had a thick accent, smoked a pipe, and at first talked about his "beloved" city of Vienna. He sat in a leather chair in front of a window that overlooked the American Embassy, the flag flapping in the wind. I sat in an orange vinyl chair from the 1970s. He looked a bit like my deceased grandfather, which added to the dramatic effect of the situation. *Was I suffering trauma?*

The Austrian advised me to return home, to my twin brother. "Start life again," he commenced. "Get a Master's Degree. What you really need is to forget this traveling nonsense. The girl, she only wants papers to travel to America."

It all felt too ridiculous, too surreal. I was speechless and one breath from voicing my true opinion. *Why don't you go back to Vienna, you patronizing bastard?* I breathed slowly, got up, and walked out.

When the Foreign Minister of Morocco caught wind of what had happened in Marrakesh, he mentioned the incident to the King of Morocco, Mohammed VI, who at the time had happened to be visiting President George W. Bush in the United States.

The charges were dropped. It was as if nothing had happened. Maybe George W. Bush had said something on my behalf. The Peace Corps office in Rabat told me to sign papers saying the whole incident was my fault, and "not due to a lack of cultural training."

Later, I figured the Peace Corps wanted to prevent a lawsuit. I wanted to forget the whole mess. I signed. The next volunteer group arriving the following month would receive not only the regular lecture on how to use a condom that took place in every training session, but also how not to "bisou," or kiss, in public—especially in Marrakesh.

Soon after, the Peace Corps office sent me deep into the High Atlas Mountains south of Marrakesh. At least there, I would keep out of trouble.

As a kid, I had always wanted to be a superhero. Now, I had become an icon of misbehavior. Stories flooded the foreign community: this naive volunteer learned the hard way how not to act in an Islamic country.

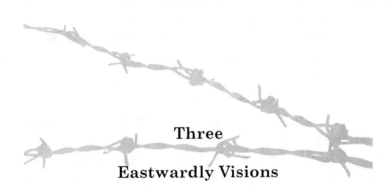

Three

Eastwardly Visions

24 August 1979

BEYOND THE tightly latched infirmary doors, Azeddine stood; the world he knew would soon be gone forever. He realized that the false security the infirmary walls provided would come crashing down. A total of twelve patients, Head Nurse Omar, Dr. Ahmed, and himself remained in the infirmary. The other two nurses had fled to the commanders' quarters in hopes of escaping with someone else bold enough to leave. Azeddine wondered if they'd made it.

The ensuing battle blended vivid colors in Azeddine's mind. Another explosive burst, which seemed just a few feet outside the walls, rang deep inside his ears. Gunshots echoed in the distant hills. Only war produced such a refrain that beat to the rhythm of distress. As blood heavily flowed and clotted within the infirmary's walls, he felt the bulging aneurysm was about to explode. Images of his own hands covered in thick blood shot through his head.

Smoke began to saturate the clinic. The stench of burnt rubber filled the corridor. Guns fired. The doors flew open.

"Get down! Hide!" Ahmed looked around the room, covered his head, bent low, and ran into the adjacent room. Nurse Omar followed him. Azeddine didn't know where to run.

He ran toward the beds he had aligned earlier. He thought about pushing them into the corridor, but it was the only way in or out of the infirmary. He had nowhere to hide the patients. Azeddine had to react. *I can't let them die!* He found a small gurney folded up against a far wall. If he had he seen it earlier, he would have used it. He decided to crouch down behind it for cover.

The smoke became thicker. If he hunkered down, he'd not only be able to hide but also to breathe a little easier below the smoke.

He saw a patient gaze over at him. His shaking hands gripped his head as he bent lower. "Allah, Allah maana" Azeddine repeated. Allah is with us.

Pressed against the cloth, he could see out into the room. From his angle, he was well hidden and all the patients were within sight.

Three of the attackers entered the room, turned, and then left. From the SADR flags on their arms, he knew they were members of the Polisario, an Algerian-backed militant group. The strange-sounding Hassani tongue echoed through the waiting room.

Many claimed Tuareg lineage. Their ancestors had traded and controlled the trans-Saharan trade routes through the Sahara Desert once upon a time. They had survived the Sahara for centuries. In the 1970s, countless fled from Western Sahara into Algeria as refugees, becoming rebels, gaining military know-how from Algerian leaders. Their mission: to rid Western Sahara of every outsider, including Moroccans, and to establish their own state.

Two of the men re-entered. They wore bright blue gondoras resembling flowing gowns of tissue paper the color of the Mediterranean Sea. Maybe they were the leaders of the group. Their gondoras allowed for the easy concealment and drawing of weapons, whether sword, knife, or gun. Indigo turbans encircled their heads.

Another soldier came into the room. He stared at the helpless patients as other members entered carrying Kalashnikovs; one had a pistol. The injured lying on the beds had no chance. They would become the prey of these scavengers.

"You didn't die," said one of the guerilla fighters in Darija so the patients would understand, "so we came to finish the job." Two of them approached the patients. Azeddine watched from behind the folded gurney, biting down on the cloth covering the small mattress.

One of the Polisario soldiers put his gun up to the first patient's temple. The patient's eyes widened as his hands flew up in the air; a crimson stream poured out onto the white pillow.

The same killer shot each remaining patient the same way. Azeddine covered his ears and bit down harder. His chest felt like it was going to explode. The last patient in line kept convulsing after he'd been shot.

Blood spilled down his face, smearing his cracked lips. He began to gurgle his own blood. The patient grabbed his head, shrieking in agony.

"This hamar won't die. Finish him off!"

One of the soldiers pointed his Kalashnikov at the bleeding man.

Azeddine thought he heard the patient utter his name; fear stabbed him like jagged glass. He only had a few seconds until his discovery and imminent death. He uncovered his ears and heard the noise of guns and machinery outside. The earth trembled beneath him and the walls shook. The supply shelves and tables toppled to the ground.

Azeddine's legs went numb. His mind wanted to purge everything he'd witnessed. Different Polisario soldiers came in and counted the bodies. They made sure each one was dead. Azeddine watched as they entered and checked the heartbeat of each jeefa, a corpse no longer containing its soul. The soldiers turned, laughed, and then departed.

Azeddine felt death's dark soul encase his body. He roamed in its layer, hiding in the shadows. He spun in and out of reality, gripping his head, looking out into the room of lost souls. He lay beneath the surface of darkness. It pulled him in. He became part of its coagulate being, drowning in its thickness. Visions of his father whirled through his mind. He longed to be near him, to kneel beside him and pray eastward toward Mecca one last time before death captured his spirit. Such lucid, painful visions he had never known before that time.

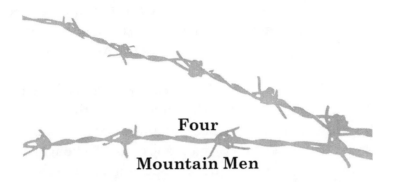

Four

Mountain Men

Early summer 2002

IN THE mountains south of Marrakesh, Brahim sat on a bright-red, plastic rug with blue mosaic designs inside the mud hut. He would be a part of my new Moroccan host family during my stay. Before my arrival that day, like a Sherpa he carried a door up a winding mountain trail for three hours so that I would have a door to my room. He somehow made it clear to me in his Berber language, "I want your stay here to be comfortable."

After all the commotion about my ordeal in Marrakesh, I wasn't ready. The same day I arrived, I felt like I was going to have a mental breakdown. Too much to handle, I re-packed my backpack and headed down the mountain trail lined with opuntia.

In a hotel that night, I dreamed of Essaouira. I would head there the next day. Sun. Wind. Escape. Freedom.

After I got off the rickety bus, a Moroccan family who said they had a room to rent immediately pinpointed me. Essaouira was magical. However, relaxing on pristine beaches was not what I had come to Morocco to do. It was just another drop in the sea of endless days that became my short time of service in Morocco.

Returning to the High Atlas after a few weeks, I decided I would give my stay in the mountains with Brahim another fresh start. He had put a new window in my room with screening to keep bugs out. We bought a mattress together at the weekly, open-air market, called the souk. He wanted to carry that up, too, on his head, but we opted for the big Mitsubishi dump truck that the villagers piled into each market day.

Mostly the female villagers carried potatoes and onions in bright purple or dark black meeka, plastic bags. One man ahead of us smiled at Brahim and waved our way as the truck bounced up and down. He had one gold molar on the left side, and small sharp black points for front teeth.

The village had mud-brick homes with flat roofs. Plastic stuck out of the ends of each corner, which revealed how they kept rain from seeping through and gravel was thrown on top to keep the plastic from flying away. The huts sat side by side and had no glass in the windows, only wooden or tin shutters.

Off in the distance were perfectly flat circles of dirt surrounding a singular wooden pole. After much pointing and gesturing, I learned that these spots are where mules, donkeys, or the rare horse husked wheat, barley, and oats from their chaffs each season. Tied to the center pole, the animals worked all day long with a Berber farmer alongside, urging them with whistles, chants, and clicks of the tongue.

Beyond this and some harvesting of walnuts, cherries, and apples at various intervals throughout the year, copious troupes of these mountain men hung out much of the day. Bent-over elderly ladies, their daughters and granddaughters walked by with piles of winter wheat tied on their backs for their animals. The men squawked at the women for tea "and don't forget the sheeba!"–a local absinth. Following, the men might throw a rock or two at the chickens. Work or the lack thereof didn't seem to bother the men all that much.

On the surface, women and men lived completely separate lives. While the Berbers are known for their kindness and were neighborly to any passerby, the weight of the Berber's existence sits literally on the women's backs and shoulders. From childrearing to preparing meals to pasturing the animals, the women spend sunrise to sunset and beyond completing the day's chores.

A good portion of my (and the women's) morning was spent filling sought-after plastic bottles, old oil containers, or used gas cans with potable water from a spring. The source near my house flowed out of a gutter contraption made of sticks and thick green leaves.

Hygiene in the Western sense wasn't easy to maintain. Bathroom practices were a whole other game. I'd have to head to an outer shed where baby goats bleated for attention. While there was no toilet, per se, I'd squat and aim into a hole of eight inches in diameter. The stuff landed into a lower level where a cow or two were kept.

Learning to understand Tashelheit, or the local

Berber dialect, wasn't difficult. I knew I had a good grasp of the language when I could finally understand what Brahim had been trying to explain to me slowly for months. He wanted to let me know how he had begotten eight children; his message was to the effect:

"Mountain men are strong. We aren't like those weaker men in the cities. Berbers in the mountains are the best lovers."

He also detailed how he had prostrated his wife in their meager kitchen to prove his manhood. *Was this mountain-man humor or something more primitive?* I wasn't sure. It probably wouldn't go over well back home, I thought.

Because of the altitude, when the rest of the country had rain, there was snow in the village. Even in June, the snow fell lightly. The stunning view of the river cutting through the Ourika valley 150 feet below painted a pristine picture that competed with any Ansel Adams portrayal, what Byron would label as sublime.

Many were scared of the river, however, with good reason. Hundreds of people had perished years prior when a surprising rain came in late summer and didn't stop. The floodwaters washed away mud villages, goats, and workers and campers who were close to its banks. It was one of Morocco's worst natural catastrophes. The government consequently installed solar-powered flood stations. If water levels escalated, the radios would automatically contact rescue units. I wasn't sure who these *units* would be. At my height above the valley, I wasn't worried about flooding as much as rock or mudslides.

In passing, I heard of another Peace Corps volunteer

who was stationed in the town around the bend, one hill over (which is how the local Berbers give directions). The neighboring villagers said he didn't come out of his house. This made me wonder. He left a few months later.

Brahim wanted to show me off to everyone around. His community now had one of these motatawayas, or volunteers, of their very own. They would make me pronounce "emiks emik, agrom, agrom" repeatedly in their Berber dialect for a laugh. The locals never tired of hearing me constantly repeat "little by little" and "bread, bread." The concept of animal or people cruelty didn't exist in these parts.

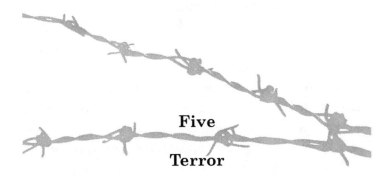

Five

Terror

24 August 1979

AZEDDINE WAS on a kind of mental cruise control. The room had an unusual feeling to it, resonating war off its walls, yet soundless within.

A Polisario soldier entered the room. Hiding for over a half hour in his corner barricade, Azeddine crouched in shock as the militant soldier took the first dead patient—the one with his leg blown off—and tugged him off the bed; he fell like a bag of cement. The Polisario fighter dragged the body along with the blood-ridden sheets out into the corridor. Still hidden behind the cot, Azeddine watched horrified as the same soldier came back into the room, folded the gurney, and wheeled it out into the corridor.

They were stealing the beds; the bodies were merely hindrances to their looting. Another thump. Two more soldiers entered. They tossed the rest of the bodies off the beds, and dragged the beds into the corridor.

Laughing, a few Polisario soldiers entered the storage room. Dr. Ahmed and Head Nurse Omar were still hiding there. Azeddine wondered if they'd be discovered. A few seconds later, the Polisario soldiers ran out of the room, holding boxes of medicine.

A few minutes later, even more soldiers came in to help empty out the storage room. Shelves clanked to the ground. Glass shattered. "Ajee, daba!"

Dr. Ahmed and Nurse Omar were shoved out of the medical storage room. Blood gushed from Ahmed's nose. They were still alive.

As they were dragged outside, no shots were fired. Azeddine couldn't hear anything. He wondered where they were being taken. He couldn't bear to think about the possibility of their impending deaths. Two Polisario vigilantes reentered and made off with the rest of the infirmary's precious reserves.

Azeddine still hadn't been discovered. Thoughts of his own survival loomed in the forefront of his mind. Once they were all gone, he would come out from behind the gurney. He would then see the catastrophic remains of Lebouirate and find Ahmed and Omar, who might have escaped the clutches of death. They'd be waiting for him amid the rubble and dead bodies.

The smoke dissipated, providing less of a shield than previously. Why hadn't they noticed the only bed, the lonely cot in the corner that hadn't been plundered?

Sweat ran down Azeddine's forehead. Luck, perhaps, was on his side.

Two thug-like Polisario soldiers advanced toward the gurney. "Lahassan, Lahassan, come."

A new surge of fear pierced the young doctor's

body. Lahassan looked at the empty cot. He slowly approached it, then stopped and pulled out his hand-gun. Azeddine crouched down even more and covered his head. He tried to slow his breathing. Something struck him. The black gel-like liquid of death that he'd felt before pulled him again. "Allah Akbar," he slurred repeatedly. "Allah Ak—".

"Stand up, puta," Lahassan barked in Spanish, Western Sahara's second language.

Azeddine was motionless. His body was limp, and he felt blood run down the side of his cheek. It was warm and strangely comforting. With hatred in their eyes, the two ruffians yanked him up by the arms.

Lahassan kicked Azeddine in the stomach and pinned the gun hard into his temple. The two held his slack body. Lahassan grabbed Azeddine by the hair, now matted with blood, and asked, "Doctor?"

Azeddine nodded slowly.

"No puedo matarte!" He couldn't kill someone so valuable.

Azeddine groaned. The soldiers grabbed Azeddine by the elbows and carried him out, his feet trailing behind. Lahassan spat on the ground in front of him.

His blood streaking the floor, Azeddine feared seeing his slain comrades. In his mind, the fountain in the corridor spouted the blood of the innocent. His murdered patients were in a row on the floor. Bloody sheets were haphazardly thrown over their stained, half-naked bodies. The two nurses who had tried earlier to flee lay on the floor; one of their bare legs protruded from the sheet. Azeddine retched in pain, vomiting as they carried him around the bodies of the massacred.

He wiped his mouth with his forearm. He wanted to remain conscious to see if he could spot the bodies of Ahmed and Omar.

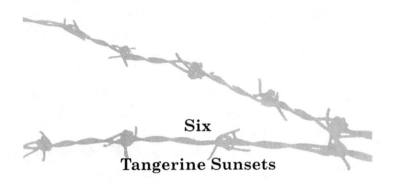

Six
Tangerine Sunsets

Summer 2002

SANAE AND I kept in touch. Sending phone messages to each other, I stood atop my mud-thatched roof in the middle of the Ourika Valley, held the phone up toward the sky, and pressed the green send key.

I learned the Berber language better, thanks to my host dad. He was proud of my progress and his sundrenched face glowed as I spoke his tongue.

When I'd go to Rabat, Sanae and I spent hours at the French Club, one of the only locations where we could get away and talk openly. Mountain living was becoming easier, but I still felt awkward about serving under an organization where I felt a strange paranoia that bordered on Orwellian.

Wanting an alternative way of staying in the country, I submitted my résumé to a few different English academies offering teaching jobs. Upon my initial request, one quality English institute in Rabat quickly said they had no further openings. The next morning, however, the director called and said that in fact a teacher was needed. It was sealed. I'd stay in Morocco, hopefully forgetting or at least feeling better about my personal issues with the Peace Corps. I wouldn't be able to stay in the mountains with Brahim and listen to his jokes about having more children, but I'd be able to stay in Morocco nonetheless.

"Field Termination" is what the government called quitting volunteer service. They offered me a one-way plane ticket to Washington D.C. *Did they really care?*

My relationship with Sanae fizzled. We couldn't regain what we had lost before the incident in Marrakesh. It was a sad parting, but we vowed to remain friends.

In the spring of 2003, a conflict thousands of miles away meant that all Peace Corps Volunteers serving in Morocco (or Jordan, the only Arab-Muslim countries where Peace Corps operates) would be pulled out of the country. With their current service status upgraded to "RPCV" (Returned Peace Corps Volunteer), many of my friends were yanked from the country they did not wish to leave. Peace Corps Morocco wanted to take every precaution that a conflict over a thousand miles away did not ripple negatively into North Africa; George W. Bush planned to finish what his father had started. Another Iraq War commenced, an event to which a majority of the world objected.

It was at this time that I visited Ifrane, Morocco. I longed for nature, something similar to Brahim's pastoral home, and the freeing mountains. With its Swiss-like appeal and unbelievable cedar forests, it was a magical town that beckoned me to stay. It was different from the High Atlas, but still had that common denominator shared by mountain locales.

I talked to the director of Al Akhawayn, an English-speaking university, and we agreed upon the job, an after-school activities director. I would be planning sports and trips to keep the students who lived in the dormitories busy after school.

By the end of that school year, I had gotten used to handling many of Morocco's most privileged yet needy youth who attended the school. Once our roles were defined, the students and I got along well. They were normal kids who needed teachers, mentors, and most often someone to listen.

During the fall semester, a surprisingly well-mannered student named Amine talked to me about a friend of his family who hadn't been home for 25 years. *Twenty-five years?* That grabbed my attention. This man had been his father's friend. They had even studied to be doctors together.

As I walked home that night, I thought about this man. *Would I be like him? Would I not return home for a long time? Why had he been away for so long? Was he in search of himself, of something greater? Where had he gone?*

Amine was not only intelligent for his age, but also possessed a patience and maturity rare for an adolescent in any country. He told me that this family friend would be visiting on the weekend, and I was welcome to join them. I wasn't sure why I had this fascination with someone I had only heard about in passing, but I accepted the invitation. I would join him and his father for sweet-mint tea and perhaps beghrir, a small, spongy, honey-soaked crepe.

At 11 a.m., we were sitting at tables outside a café somewhere in the central part of Fez. A dry breeze blew dust up from the street. Fez was only an hour from Ifrane but a world apart in comparison. A gold Toyota Corolla pulled up. A lady, who had her head covered but not her face, stepped out. Another man, somewhat short with grayish remnants of hair and sideburns, was with her. Amine's father, a doctor who looked the part down to the fine suit, hugged the man. They went through the long introductions, asking about family, friends, life, and health. Amine's father lightly shook the lady's hand.

My Arabic wasn't that good. I had remembered some Berber from the mountain village, and was learning French from a *Berlitz* conversation book.

"Salam alaykoom," the doctor wearing a brown coat and sweater said as I shook his hand.

"Mucharfeen," I repeated. He looked normal to me. He didn't look like he had been gone for decades. In fact, he seemed clean-cut, calm, together. He sat beside Amine's father while Amine translated. The lady who had driven was his sister. They ordered nuss-nuss, half-milk, half-coffee.

His name was Azeddine. He chatted with Amine's father as if they had met every Saturday for the past twenty years. Azeddine's brown coat lay behind him on the chair. I noticed a tattoo on his arm, which was rare for a Moroccan. Only criminals, from my understanding, had tattoos on the upper part of their forearms. Amine said that Azeddine had a card that showed he was in the military, at war, that he could take public transportation and receive free medical aid. He showed us his card.

Morocco at war, with whom? Everyone seemed to be at peace. The Peace Corps never would have come if there had been a war.

At home that night, the air was surprisingly hot, miserable. I opened the windows and let the breeze come through. Small pieces of the blue wallpaper broke off and scattered over the floor. I trudged across the cold floor, found my slippers, and sat on the couch. I tried writing a letter. All I could think about was Azeddine.

Amine was able to arrange another meeting. My French was passable, but I couldn't handle a conversation alone. Maybe Amine would translate.

Agreed—we'd meet on Saturday. During that week, Azeddine had written 90 pages of illegible notes (quite normal for a doctor in any country, I suspected) about his time away. We met in Amine's living room. His mother brought out cookies, Cornes de Gazelle. "Good for men with hard-to-please ladies," they teased.

After talking for hours, my brain was full. Another sleepless night. I was ravenous for more. Azeddine intrigued me. His calmness of mind and the eagerness in his eyes hooked me into his tale that spanned half a lifetime.

In two months time—surprising Amine, Azeddine, and myself—I didn't need a full-time translator anymore. I was scarcely able to speak, but I was competent enough to understand what Azeddine was saying. We kept meeting regularly. Somehow, he trusted me. His family welcomed me, let me sleep over after a long day's talk, and fed me.

"Il faudra dire—We must tell the world what happen in Sahara."

"Yes, it's true," I exhaled. "I am going to try. I'll try to…" It felt like we had known each other in some other lifetime.

Azeddine excused himself, laid his small, rectangular prayer carpet on the floor facing east. He bowed, stood, kneeled, and pressed his forehead to the ground. His unbroken devoutness to his religion astounded me.

We do have to tell the world. We would have to tell everyone about the atrocities occurring deep in the Sahara sands. "Bismillah Rahman oo Rahim…." I heard Azeddine whispering, "In the name of Allah, most gracious, most merciful…. " Something of an epiphany struck; the prayer call, the tangerine sunset, Azeddine, the allure of Morocco: my understanding had only begun.

Seven

Indigo Abyss

24 August 1979

PUDDLES FORMED around the bodies. Blood-stained footprints like warm tar marked the movement of the killers.

With his pistol firmly pressed against Azeddine's back, Lahassan shoved Azeddine forward as the other two soldiers dragged him out of the infirmary. Azeddine wasn't blinded by the sunlight, but choked by the coal-black billows filling the sky.

The small village of Lebouirate had turned into an inferno; demons danced in the havoc. A camel had been burned alive. Dead animals, goats and sheep, lay all around. Underfed stray dogs, once lounging in the morning sun or shading themselves during the intense afternoon heat, had also fallen victim to the slaughter.

"Ils ont perdu leur raison," Azeddine said in his mother's small living room as he relayed the horrific scene in what would become one of our many interviews together. It was like they were all going crazy. The life that was once Lebouirate panicked in its own destruction.

A tapestry,
deep scarlet velvet, green star
lifeless soldiers, forever etched

On the canvas of Azeddine's memory, there were sallow splotches of black and gray, borderless bodies lying on the rocky ground. Civilians mutilated beyond recognition—an atrocious, never-ending nightmare.

The Polisario fighters dragged Azeddine even faster. The pistol was still tightly pinned against his back.

To his left were two slain bodies. He didn't recognize them. One was an ill-fated soul who'd been tied to a tree. Set alight, his body had been eaten alive by fire. His flesh was purplish-black. Smoke steamed off of his clothes that hung smoldering from his arms and legs in crisp shreds. His mouth was agape. His head protruded stiffly out into the air, hair burnt in patches — the agony of his death frozen on his face.

Next to the burned victim was the body of a man Azeddine had recently befriended. He had been one of the best marksmen; his head was now severed from his body.

"Hakim!"

Azeddine put his hand on the wooden table we sat around many afternoons. "What a servant of Allah ... " Azeddine said in French and then mumbled something in Arabic, shaking his head.

Hakim's head lay sideways in the dirt, just a few feet

away from his body. The blood had drained into the ground. His eyes would never again possess their green sharpness. His thick black hair was moist and clumpy, resembling honey, not blood.

Azeddine mentioned something about talking to Hakim before the attack. I couldn't quite make out what he meant. He went on to say that Ahmed had witnessed something in the small village before all of this atrocity. *Had Ahmed seen something as gruesome as this? Was his too a tale of survival?* I had so much to ask, but Azeddine's eyes asked me to refrain.

Part Two: The Desert Within

20 May 1973: El-Khanga Attack

El Khanga was a small Spanish military outpost in the northeast of Western Sahara. It had a small garrison of troops. The Polisario group consisted of seven men, among them the Front's secretary general, Luali Mustafa Sayed. The attacking group relied mainly on the advantage of surprise since they were outnumbered and outgunned. The garrison was occupied almost instantly after the attack had begun. This small raid marked the beginning of a long armed struggle that Polisario fought against the colonial power, Spain, and later against the invasion of Western Sahara by Morocco and Mauritania.

- Polisario Homepage

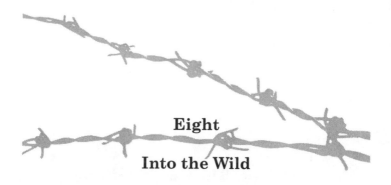

Eight

Into the Wild

SURVIVAL IN the Peace Corps meant following unwritten rules. A week gone by without occurrence was good news. Most often freak accidents were avoided, but smaller incidents are what got volunteers into trouble.

Daily survival meant something as simple as remembering to shut off the butane-gas tank that connects to the stove. For others, survival was making sure you didn't get caught smoking or, especially, stashing portions of the country's vast supply of hashish in your small mud hut.

The Peace Corps system, at least in Morocco, was strangely set up for failure. It was as if the US government wanted kudos for sending their citizens abroad to help their Muslim neighbors, but the main objective was often blurry. One country director would replace another.

The stories that we not only heard but also lived each

day surpassed the imagination. Walking three hours in the Moroccan countryside, known as the "bled," to buy vegetables was a weekly event. It was as normal as going to the mall back home. Volunteers who lived with the Berber tribes were considered Berbers. Many dressed like those with whom they lived and worked: bright multi-colored jackets, random scarves, and tight plastic sandals were the norm.

Later, working at Al Akhawayn University gave me time to reflect on my short time as a volunteer. My hours spent with Azeddine, coupled with writing, were *my* Morocco now. I cherished it. Only when I was with him or absorbed in his tale did I feel any balance.

The significance of my empathy for Azeddine's plight hit hard when I visited the underground prison outside the fortified city walls of Meknes. The tyrannical Sultan, Moulay Ismail, had once chained up slaves below this city's ancient ground. These slaves endured the sweltering days and bitter-cold nights, much like the prisoners held in the Sahara.

The snowy winter finally gave way to spring in Ifrane, the mountain village that was now home in the Middle Atlas. To my surprise, mushrooms, known as Morels, were sold at the local market for next to nothing. My brother and I grew up hunting these same mushrooms with our father. Our dad often carried one small arrow from his archery set, claiming that when he threw it, it magically pointed to an area of mushrooms. Once it landed, all you had to do was look around. It always worked.

I didn't have that arrow with me now, so I didn't have

much luck finding them when I hiked in the forest. But the Berber shepherds of the area were gifted, returning with garbage bags full. To be truthful, I bought some from the town's central market and told my new girl-friend that I had found a few.

My father's arrow could point us and lead us in the right direction, but we'd always have to look a little harder—dig a little deeper. My time with Azeddine was similar. His story led and pointed me to some unbeknownst place. I wondered who else would listen and where this tale would lead me.

Azeddine and I started meeting more often. In his mother's rectangular living room, lined with cushions decorated with fine brocade, we'd conduct our interviews. Azeddine described in a combination of languages what he'd experienced. His voice cracked as he recollected the events of his capture.

The Polisario insurgents dragged him over the rugged paths. When he gained his balance, he attempted running to keep upright and alongside his captors. The soldiers threw him back onto the ground and tied his wrists securely behind him. Fighter jets thundered in the distance. The men pointed toward the sky, and then took off running, full speed, lugging Azeddine even faster over rocks, through sand and dirt.

"…jets was les Mirage Fighters from the France," Azeddine said in broken English as he wrote out the name of the fighter planes before me on a pad of paper he carried with him. His mother entered and brought us mint tea. She made sure we stayed well supplied, not quite understanding our mixed-language conversations.

The planes flashed overhead, randomly dropping napalm and phosphorous bombs, shooting haphazardly at no one target. The two rebels dragging Azeddine shoved him to the ground. Each on one knee, they shot their Kalashnikovs into the sky toward the jets. The rescue had come too late.

Lahassan, the leader of the raid, turned and glared down at Azeddine, who couldn't make out the leader's features, except for his high, shadowy cheekbones and indigo turban that caused his sweat to turn dark blue as it dripped down his face.

Lahassan swung a striking blow to Azeddine's head.

"J'ai vu noir," his head moving loosely, his prisoner's eyes widening and slowly closing. He saw only black.

When Azeddine awakened from the blow, he lay on his stomach, legs now tied to his wrists with wire behind his back. He found himself in some type of 4x4 jeep. The vehicle bounced sharply over the terrain. A gnawing pain replaced the darkness. Something beside him snorted. A goat was equally bound beside him. It watched nervously with its yellowish eyes at each of Azeddine's futile movements.

In the distance, the bombing of Lebouirate continued. The village was annihilated. The clunking of the 4x4 muffled the sounds of the atrocity behind them.

"Nobody around," Azeddine recalled as he looked around the room as if he were looking for someone. "Ahmed probablement était tué dehors l'infimirie," he thought aloud. Ahmed was maybe killed outside the clinic.

Azeddine stood and stretched his back. He began

63

pacing intensely around the living room table, shaking his head as he questioned himself. He didn't remember hearing any gunshots. He reassured himself. Nor did he see their bodies on top of the bloody mound of corpses outside the emergency ward.

Back in the 4x4, the inimical creature beside him reeked of piss; it delivered a spring-loaded jolt into Azeddine's right hamstring. Pain surged through him. Even with the goat's hind legs tied, it could buck. Azeddine tried to scoot away, rolling onto his side to keep it at bay.

Lahassan stood over him while the 4x4 bounced over the jagged terrain. He had one arm wrapped firmly around the truck's roll bar while he swiveled his head around like a periscope to view the destruction behind them. Azeddine shut his eyes and tried to keep as far away from Lahassan's stare and the goat's thrusts as he could.

No rescue came. They stopped at a small oasis. It was about a half-acre of sporadic desert brush and dried date palms. The area wasn't fertile, but barren, just like the rest of the place. Azeddine watched through a small gunshot hole in the side of the 4x4 as the vigilantes sat beneath the inadequate shade of the palms, built a small fire, and made tea. For a moment, the goat remained reticent. The scorching August sun of the desert was rising toward its mid-day pinnacle.

Lahassan walked toward the back of the jeep. Now that Azeddine had a better look, Lahassan's face wasn't as sweaty, but it was still blotched dark blue from the trickling dye of his turban and oily black with what looked like motor grease. Lahassan exhaled smoke from his cigarette and didn't say anything. He reached down, untied Azeddine's black military boots, and tugged them off.

Through the same gunshot hole, Azeddine watched Lahassan casually walk away with the boots underneath his left arm, puffing away at his cigarette.

Visions of his patients' bodies beneath blood-drenched sheets, stained the color of dried cherry juice, flashed through Azeddine's mind. His captors walked back toward him. As they started the engine, diesel fumes exuded out the back. They drove over innumerable bumps, rocks, and sparse sandy dunes.

These Polisario vigilantes lived and even thrived in the desert. They could easily navigate wherever they wanted, eluding whomever they wished. At nightfall, they'd utilize the magnificent night sky, reclusive stars, and mysterious nomadic paths to escape deeper into this forgotten wasteland that they claimed as their rightful homeland.

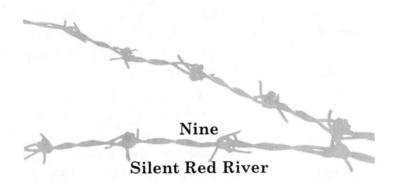

Nine

Silent Red River

25 August 1979

THAT NIGHT, the Polisario guerillas stopped the 4x4 and took turns sleeping. Azeddine slept a disturbed, painful sleep. He thirsted for anything and even tried swallowing his own saliva. The intense smell of dried goat piss saturated his clothes.

"Bismillah, don't forget to bless Allah before your throat is slit," Lahassan grumbled before checking Azeddine's tied wrists. Azeddine felt like an animal in line for slaughtering.

At dawn the next morning, the vigilantes began their day. They drank tea and ate bread, which was wrapped in a handkerchief and had been stored in the glove compartment. They were still joyous, celebrating a murderous communion.

"Je suis assoiffé et affamé!" Azeddine recalled. I wasn't sure if he was talking about being thirsty during his capture or now, as I smelled the lunch that his mother and sister were preparing in the small tiled kitchen. They often prepared quite a feast on the weekends. Ironically, I could also smell freshly baked bread. Bread in Morocco, or especially in Islam, is the food of Allah. Bread is sustaining, life giving. Moroccans eat it with nearly every meal, using it at dinner to soak up saucy meat stews.

At Azeddine's, like anywhere, one eats with the right hand. Remnants of greasy food can be dripping off your chin or smeared on your clothes or the white tablecloth and no one will take a second look. But if you eat with your left hand, you'll bring on long stares of abomination: the right hand is for food, while the left is used to clean up after using the bathroom.

"So I want water. So hungry," Azeddine repeated.

Tied up in the back of the 4x4, he feared he would die if he didn't get some nourishment. The militants untied his legs for a few minutes, and he was able to climb out of the truck bed. The hot sand penetrated his socks; his legs felt like they had no blood flowing through them. He tried remaining in the shade of the truck. One of the drivers held his water bag up to Azeddine's mouth and gave him a drink for the first time since his capture the day before.

His stomach growled. He watched as they shared the bread with one another, dipping it in olive oil that they poured from an old can. The smell of it wafted toward him. The driver picked up the heel, walked over to Azeddine and thrust it at him. It landed on his lap as he sat against the back tire.

"Shokran," Azeddine whispered hoarsely.

The goat no longer budged in the back of the 4x4, but it breathed heavily with intermittent spasms and grunts.

After about three more hours of driving, the man behind the wheel brought the jeep to an abrupt stop and left the engine running. Azeddine understood one word, "Mahbes."

Moroccans do not often visit Mahbes. At one point in time, it was known as the gateway into Algeria.

"The dry river is Saguia el-Hamra, name in Arabia," Azeddine said, taking a pencil and spelling it out for me, making me repeat the name no less than five times, proud each time I got some nuance of the accent.

It was the Red River's Path. This parched riverbed, which extends east from Laayoune and connects into Tindouf, Algeria, marks the northernmost region of Western Sahara's border. I tried asking Azeddine to give me the exact coordinates of the Red River and the upper-boundary of the desert, but he could only point to the general vicinity on our rudimentary Michelin map. He told me I'd need to get a detailed map of the region in Rabat, but to be careful since it might raise some degree of suspicion if I were to go asking around for topographical maps of Western Sahara in government offices.

The Polisario weren't going into the southern section of Western Sahara, known only as the Rio de Oro, or River of Gold, like Azeddine had thought when he was first captured.

"No. We go straight to the Algèrie." Azeddine had also guessed wrongly that his captors might head for

Ad-Dakhla in Western Sahara, a name given to the southern border town due to the possibilities of early traders obtaining African gold dust there. He had theorized that they'd try to escape through Mauritania, but that wasn't so.

The post where Azeddine was taken was actually quite a distance from the Moroccan-controlled Mahbes. Where he was now was less than a ghost town; it was more of a ghost station. The place was made up of one gendarme station and two garages. An officer, dressed in gray with a black belt and a dark blue hat, stepped out of his station. Lahassan jumped out of the 4x4. Azeddine noticed Lahassan was wearing the boots he'd stolen from him the previous day. Lahassan walked toward the gendarme and gave him a hug with two swift pats on the back. The gendarme returned the motion.

"Well, I caught a Moroccan," Lahassan said as he smoked another cigarette.

The officer walked up, peered into the back of the 4x4, and spoke in Arabic, making sure Azeddine heard.

"Which one do I get to eat?" the gendarme asked.

"Take your pick."

"Let me see. Can either one of them change a tire?"

"One will taste better than the other."

"Let me take *him* to the garage."

Lahassan's driver jumped out of the jeep, untied Azeddine, and forced him out. The gendarme walked Azeddine, hobbling over the rocks without his boots, toward a lone building.

Azeddine rubbed his wrists that were raw and covered with dried blood from the abrasive wire. He wasn't sure what was going to happen.

"Lma, afek." Water, please.

"I'll get you water, klb, but first you'll have to earn it."

"Shokran, Sidi."

Azeddine entered the dark garage. It took a moment for his eyes to adjust. The gendarme mentioned that he needed him to take a tire off of a rim. The job would have to be done immediately. The patrolman left him alone, slamming the door shut behind him. A gap where the roof and walls met provided a small beam of light where dust particles shone in midair.

Azeddine looked at the massive tire that lay on the dirt floor. Belonging to a tractor or some type of military machinery, the grimy tire had a crowbar leaning against it that would be insufficient to handle such a large job. Azeddine attempted to work the bar around the edges of the rim, but his usual robustness had been severely weakened from the trauma in Lebouirate and his hunger. However, he was content to have some freedom in movement that allowed him to loosen up his stiff muscles.

Exhaustion overtook him easily. He sat down on the tire and rubbed his wrists again. Azeddine peered into a dark corner where he heard something move. On closer inspection, it looked as if a rat was checking out an empty old tool bench built into the corner. What his mind thought was a rat quickly became the shape of a thin man, who stood up and dusted off his raggedy blue coveralls. Azeddine stared in amazement, wondering where this person had come from.

"He had long barbe!" Azeddine declared pointing to

my chin as if I were the one with the beard. Azeddine adjusted himself on his sofa excitedly. The phone rang. He told me not to say anything. He later explained that he didn't want anyone to know we were meeting; people would get suspicious.

Perhaps he is overly paranoid? I thought to myself. In spite of this, his suspicion about the world had probably saved his life on several occasions. Although paranoia did not seem a natural trait for him, it had become an enhanced, finely tuned survival tactic.

The thin man in the garage was older than Azeddine. The man's massive gray and black beard spread down from his chin to past his collarbone. It was filled with soot and dust. His matted hair protruded out of a faded orange cap.

"Welcome to the middle of nowhere," the man said in Arabic, "Smeetee Ali."

Azeddine, still fixated on the man's beard, walked closer to him and held out his hand. "Smeetee Azeddine." He tossed the crowbar on the ground beside him. "You have the longest beard!" he blurted in Darija.

"That's why they call me Ali Baba!" he said jokingly. "Ali Baba, the one with the long beard."

Azeddine's instinct told him he could trust Ali. "I'm from Fez. Benmansour is my family name."

Ali blinked and stroked his beard with his right hand. The beard made his eyes protrude even more. "I'm from Casablanca. Where are they taking you?"

"They attacked Lebouirate and raided the village. I'm a doctor. Another doctor and I were assigned to do our military service there." Azeddine thought about Ahmed. All he could do now was hope and pray. He believed Ahmed was still alive. He'd put his concern at the feet of Allah in a silent prayer during their escape through the desert.

"This war, it's costing us all too much," Ali said, interrupting Azeddine's thoughts.

Ali walked over to the enormous tire, picked up the crowbar, grabbed a hollow metal bar that lay near an old engine, and with the metal bar over the crowbar, began prying the tire off. Azeddine joined him.

"I was captured in 1976," Ali grunted as his lips pursed from the labor. "I'm not even in the military. I'm a bulldozer operator." He shook the sweat from his brow, and then wiped it with his sleeve.

Azeddine looked around furtively, "Listen, Ali, I have to escape. Is there a—"

"Don't try it!" Ali retorted. "You have no chance. Rely on Allah. Only Allah."

Azeddine's eyes welled up as we sat on the cushions that lined the living room. The shock of the moment came back to him. He shambled into the bathroom in his mother's small pink plastic slippers. "I do wash for lunch," he said.

After lunch, Azeddine's spirits were lifted. He talked about the gendarme who brought him a canteen of water. "Lma de Paradis," he said as he smiled. It was like water from heaven.

The gendarme entered, looked at the unfinished work, and saw Azeddine and Ali together. Azeddine told Ali he'd see him again, inshallah. The officer said nothing as he escorted Azeddine out of the garage.

An oversized GMC truck with green canvas over the

back-end was parked beside the gendarme station. It had been stolen from the Moroccan forces that had obtained it from arms dealers in America. Remnants of a Moroccan flag, including a partially faded green star, remained on the driver's-side door.

Lahassan tied Azeddine's arms behind his back again. The goat was nowhere in sight.

Inside the GMC, Azeddine sat on long wooden boxes that were nailed shut. Diesel fumes permeated the bottom of the truck bed; the boxes clanked together as they drove. From inside the truck cabin, Lahassan patted his hand over his heart and waved to the patrolman as they passed.

Perhaps the officer had taken him to the garage on purpose to hear Ali's warnings. He wanted to heed Ali's advice: he should trust Allah, but the turmoil hadn't built up on him yet like it had with Ali. All Azeddine wanted was to return to his old life, which he revisited in reverie during his long forthcoming captivity.

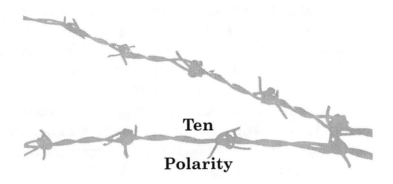

Ten

Polarity

THE YEAR before his capture, Azeddine had enjoyed the weeks bringing an end to summer, especially with his father, who was more like a brother to him than anything else. The brisk winter nights would be on their way soon, but for the time being, the dry, cool evening breeze was refreshing.

Women chatting on top of the terraces, buyers and sellers trading their wares, and mules transporting materials down interconnected alleys reflected the timbre of medieval times. Azeddine appreciated the color, contrasts, and daily life that continued on between the crumbling fortified walls.

Even though Azeddine would soon go back to medical school, these evenings with his father provided a break away from the scorching heat.

Meanwhile, Morocco was enduring unstable political times. Spain had begun mining in what the world had dubbed the "Spanish Sahara." The Spaniards discovered that this land, about the size of Colorado in the United States or Romania in Eastern Europe, incubated over ten million tons of phosphate. The Saharawi people of the land, who were fleeing into southern Algeria during these troubled times, formed the Polisario Liberation Front under Sidi Brahim Bassiri. *Polisario* is the Spanish acronym for the Frente Popular para la Liberacíon de Saguia el-Hamra y de Rio de Oro, or the Popular Front for the Liberation of the Red River's Path and the River of Gold. Receiving protection, training, and financial backing from Algeria and Libya gave the Polisario rebel force the means to stake a claim on their homeland, along with mining rights to the opulent phosphate mines.

The Polisario began their first attacks on Spanish posts in the early 1970s. Spain foresaw that the radicals were an entity to be reckoned with, so they brought in their own soldiers and navy.

Spain wasn't about to give up its supposed entitlement that easily. It had formed clear borders in the latter 1950s. This new area included the geographic coordinates of the *Rio de Oro* along the coastlines of Cape Bojador, Cape Blanco, and the northern section of Saguia el-Hamra. The access points to the Atlantic Ocean were most prized by Algeria, who was jealous of Spain's newly triumphant discovery of minerals and the ease at which it could transport the riches out of the region. The Spanish Saharan border was only a stone's throw away from Algeria and Mauritania.

The Spanish Sahara had theoretically existed for nearly a hundred years after one Emilio Bonelli, who in the middle of the 1880s, with the backing of the Sociedad Española de Africanistas y Colonistas, obtained signed treaties to the area. The Spanish government reacted in the most opportunistic way they could and soon declared a protectorate.

While Spain had gained the coastal areas, they weren't as successful at establishing their stake in the interior of its northern borders. In the early 1900s, Smara was formed and wouldn't be fully occupied until the 1930s due to the resistance of the oasis-dwelling peoples who lived there.

When Morocco gained its independence from France in 1956, the king quickly asserted his kingdom's claims to the region. Morocco repeatedly sent troops into the area, but to no avail. Once Spain officially declared the appellation of the Spanish Sahara, Morocco and Mauritania, which had also gained its independence, were furious that their rights were not recognized. Upon the discovery of phosphate in Bu Craa, the ante shot up in exponential proportions. Mining in Bu Craa didn't begin until 1972.

Spain met adversaries at every turn. The Polisario grew in number and military strength due to the region's disgruntled Saharawi inhabitants who joined their ranks. With growing international pressure for a peaceful ending, Spain affirmed that it would depart from the region by 1975, but still wanted a portion of the mining profits and certain fishing rights.

When Morocco saw that Spain would keep true to its word, King Hassan II asserted that Western Sahara was his people's land. He ran into trouble when this claim was brought formally to the International Court of Justice. The court found no substantial legal and historical ties between Morocco and the Saharan regions in question.

This decree sparked national outcry. From his Agadir post, King Hassan II called for the Green March, a peaceful demonstration involving 350,000 Moroccan men and women. Swarms rallied into what is now Western Sahara carrying only the Holy Koran and Moroccan flags, hoping to bring unity to a country on the brink of war. In the backdrop, however, intermittent clashes became frequent with the emerging power of the Polisario.

Azeddine recalled, as we sat in his sister's house discussing the '70s, how it was all "un changement de temps," a change of scenery. He discussed how he and his father had passed the time in Fez. They'd go to their favorite café, overlooking the distant hilly horizon where, in subdued whispers, everyone discussed the fate of the country and its people. A waiter brought their cafés au lait.

The sun mirrored off the archaic homes that formed this intricate labyrinth of the Fez Medina, where traders from Andalusia had once passed on their way to Timbuktu and Sub-Saharan Africa. With them, they brought gold, silver, jewelry, fine cloth, along with salt and other spices.

Turmoil in Western Sahara escalated. Within a few years, Azeddine graduated medical school. His father was ecstatic; Azeddine could see it in his smile. When his sister gave him a new necklace for graduation, his father's grin seemed to have new grooves and lines that

Azeddine had never seen before. His younger brother, who was entering middle school at the time, was a bit jealous from all the attention that came Azeddine's way.

Azeddine was thinking of starting his own medical practice. He asked his dad, half-jokingly, if he would be interested in making him special trays and plates of fine copper or silver. His dad had been in the business for years.

Some months later, as Azeddine continued to plan his future and enjoy his time with his family, he received a letter by courier. With the letter in hand, he turned past the mantel that displayed family photos, and rushed upstairs to his room. The young graduate excitedly opened a letter he hoped would contain a medical posting issued by the government.

The letter he received was dated two weeks earlier. It read: "Please report to Casablanca. You are to be placed into military service, which may not exceed nine months. Report within three days of receiving this draft notice."

The letter was supposed to be an invitation for a medical posting, not a draft.

Azeddine looked around, not wanting his mother to hear us as we discussed this scene from the past. "Chaque nuit," he said, "I hear my parents not sleeping, but talking all night." His mother and father had sadly coped with the news.

I could tell by the way his mother looked at him, her eyes longed for the years they had lost. Azeddine was much older now. A lingering half-smile would fill her face, and she'd dismiss herself from the room.

Azeddine said that after he received the letter, he took the train to Casablanca. He was used to traveling, since he had completed his medical studies in Rabat. Casablanca wasn't too far from Rabat, but in Azeddine's mind, the much noisier, metropolitan city was completely different.

Azeddine and some Royal Military Officers were taken south along the Atlantic Coast just a few weeks later. The blue water and white-crested waves helped him forget about his recently donned green uniform. He was leaving behind the beauty of Fez. He saw the world in different colors. His thoughts were scattered, the bizarre twist in his future unforeseen.

Once the cargo van he was riding in reached Agadir, a town that had seen trouble a decade earlier when a major earthquake killed thousands, he felt a peculiar loss for these people he had never known. The city was rebuilt soon after, thanks to financial contributions by Germany, who considered the town a winter haven.

Azeddine wanted to watch the "coucher de soleil" over the ocean, where Allah would mix brilliant reddish-orange clouds with shades of purple. Such were the colors that Delacroix and Matisse cherished.

The next day Azeddine was taken to the small Berber town of Tiznit. The town is admired by backpacking tourists for its jewelry shops and prized by surfers for its outlying beaches. However, he had no time to explore. Taken forty miles away to Bouzakame, he had a layover. He awaited a military helicopter that would take him to his outlying post. Ground convoy was too risky. Too many trucks had already been either blown to pieces or stolen. They'd spare the hardware but kill the driver and passengers. Within an hour, Azeddine was on his way to Lebouirate, to an unknown fate.

For the first two days in his new post, he walked around the small village in the early morning, observing its daily routines. The villagers were Moroccan and even spoke Darija rather than the common Tashelheit or Hassani. The people were different and much simpler than the people farther north. Both men and women worked, but the women worked harder. On their backs, they carried huge amounts of brush, used to make fires in their earthen stoves. Each married woman had a tattoo of two straight lines on her chin and straight parallel lines on her cheekbones. Many of the men in town were aged; their younger counterparts either joined the army or left for work in bigger cities. The children were free to run about as they pleased, but only after they carried the daily water supply in plastic containers from a small well back to their mud-houses. Afterwards, they chased baby chicks, goats, and mules.

Each afternoon, the cracked ground baked. On his second evening, he thought about going out to watch the townspeople prepare for their evening meals. He felt like a castaway on an island within a sea of sand.

As he was lacing up his boots, someone entered his small barracks. It was a lieutenant; tall, lean, with a square head that sat upon prominent but narrow shoulders. His face was genuinely handsome. At first glance, one noted trustworthiness in his eyes. His skin was darker than Azeddine's. It looked as if he had been licked by the sun, wind, and sand all at once.

"Labas?" the stranger offered. How are you? He took out a cigarette and offered it to Azeddine, who had never smoked before. Azeddine said hello, meekly stated that he didn't smoke, finished lacing, stood up, and put out his right hand.

Azeddine gripped the stranger's hand. The unlit cigarette dangled from the corner of his mouth. He seemed high-spirited yet down-to-earth. He lit his cigarette, cupping his hand around the flame. In Darija, he said, "My name's Ahmed. I'm the current doctor on base." He took two puffs. "You're here to replace me."

He didn't look like a doctor, but neither did Azeddine. "Mucharfeen." Pleased to meet you. "I'm Azeddine. I'm here to assist you. I'm supposed to be here for six months, then three months in Rabat before I get to go home."

Ahmed took a deeper puff. "I've been here for six months already and am supposed to get out of here soon. You'll get to know the townspeople at least."

"Have you served all your time here?" Azeddine looked for a chair. Not finding one, he pointed to the cot. "Have a seat."

Ahmed took the cigarette out of his mouth and brought it down to his waist so the smoke came up behind him. He didn't sit, but turned his head, blew out the smoke, and replied after a slight pause, "Not much to do around here, in this small of a village. Do you want to see the infirmary?"

"Bien sûr. Merci." Azeddine followed him outside.

The infirmary was situated to the southeast of Azeddine's barracks. As they walked, Azeddine noticed an

American GMC truck nearby. It had all sorts of antennas protruding out of the green canvas that wrapped the entire back-end.

Once inside the infirmary, Azeddine was surprised to see a little fountain in the middle of the corridor that spurted water into the air. Fountains of this kind were commonly used to help keep open-air sections of traditional Moroccan homes cool in the summer.

"For the home of feeling." Azeddine said, his English improving in the months we had spent together.

"The feeling of home," I suggested.

"Yes. Exactly."

"Selon l'Islam, we can not create images of animals or living things. We use mosaics." He drew a copy of the mosaic tiles that lined the floor below the fountain in the infirmary.

Inside the infirmary's corridor, French and Arabic newspapers lay near the waiting room chairs. The vacant walls didn't offer much in the way of art or entertainment.

Azeddine continued to describe that in a corner near the reception and sign-in desk was a cage with two rabbits: one white, one brown. Mohammed, the prophet of Islam, adored cats, but believed dogs to be unclean.

Azeddine admitted out loud that Mohammed would probably have liked rabbits.

The infirmary, at first glance, was capacious. The floors were clean, but the walls were pasty and grimy. Two posters, one written in Arabic, the other French, detailed what identification soldiers should have on them in case of an emergency. Three male nurses walked around, clipboards in hand. One was situated behind the reception desk near the rabbits. Above his head was a picture of King Hassan II in a dusty gold-painted wooden frame. The king sat on his throne surrounded by his two young sons, one on the right and the other on the left.

The nurse stood and greeted the men with a handshake. He was taller than either of them, with strong forearms and a slender body. He introduced himself as Head Nurse Omar.

To the left of the entrance was a triage room alongside the nurse's station. To the right were a consultation room with a small examination bed and a counter with supplies. Just beyond this was a small dental office. Since no dentist resided on site, it wasn't used much. Empty boxes were stacked to the ceiling, covering the dental chair. Toward the back of the infirmary was the Salle d'Hospitalisation, which held ten to twelve gurneys. Through this ward, one could directly access the pharmaceutical storage room.

Leaving the infirmary, Ahmed hailed another friend, who ran across the path to greet them both with a bisous on each cheek. Ahmed introduced the man as Hakim, the shooting instructor. Hakim had green eyes, rare in a mostly brown-eyed society, and thick brown eyebrows. He gave Ahmed a cigarette. Azeddine declined but noted Hakim always had an extra cigarette ready in his shirt pocket.

Hakim looked at Azeddine. "Have you ever shot guns before?" he asked in a Darija accent from the northern part of the country; it was funny sounding, with certain drawn-out vowel sounds at the end of words.

"Je n'aime pas l'idée," Azeddine remarked as if he

believed carrying a gun were a sin. He didn't like the idea.

Ahmed told him Hakim was the best shooting instructor in the entire upper-Sahara. Then, Ahmed revealed laughingly that he was, in fact, the only one.

The next day, which would have been Azeddine's fourth day in Lebouirate, he walked toward the infirmary. Hakim waved him over. They shook hands, exchanged a bisous, and went through the usual Moroccan greeting:

"Labas?"

"Labas. Al Hamdullah. Koolshee Bekhir?"

"Labas. Hamdullah."

Hakim went on to explain that the small village had been attacked two weeks prior by the Polisario. They had threatened the Moroccan forces and said they would have no mercy next time.

"Ahmed was here pendant l'attaque," Azeddine said to me as he relived the shock.

"Pourquoi voulaient-ils Lebouirate?" I asked trying to think of why the Polisario would want such a village located in the middle of nowhere.

"Lma," he said slowly. Water.

Azeddine related what he had learned from Hakim: Lebouirate had two of the largest water reserves near the Algerian border. They were nothing like the one in Rabonée, which the Polisario used in southwestern Algeria, but it was worth fighting to get. The Polisario soldiers had killed a handful of Moroccan soldiers who were patrolling Lebouirate, then fled. Ahmed couldn't save the soldiers. The Polisario had pinned a message in Arabic on one of the dead soldier's coats. It read: All who follow Hassan II in our land will perish. Leave at once. Don't allow your dictator to sacrifice you like worthless goats.

Hakim described that a helicopter had come to get Ahmed some days ago. His replacement, which Azeddine learned was himself, hadn't yet arrived. So, the helicopter left Ahmed standing there, bags in hand. They were to return in a week, but never did.

Later, Azeddine blamed himself. He was the reason Ahmed had stayed in the dangerous village. If Ahmed's life were taken in the second raid, Azeddine said he wouldn't forgive himself.

"Je n'ai rien pu faire." There was nothing he could do.

He hadn't decided when to come to Lebouirate. Fate or misfortune, or perhaps both, had taken over their lives.

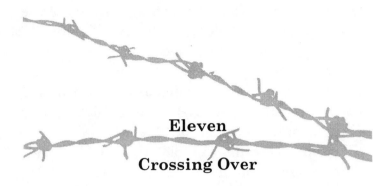

Eleven
Crossing Over

September 1979

AZEDDINE STOOD up as fast as he could when the truck came to a halt. It was dark. He couldn't see to climb out. Commotion outside the green canvas escalated.

Lahassan pounded on the canvas with his gun. "Khorj, al klb!" Come out, dog!

There was more pounding from the outside. Laughter surrounded him.

Azeddine cautiously bent his knees and tried sitting on the edge of the truck when one of Lahassan's men grabbed him by the arm, jerking him down to the ground. The gritty taste of sand filled his mouth. The distant buzz of laughter intensified.

He had managed to build up enough saliva to clean out his mouth when someone kicked him. After another swift jolt to the kidneys, he rolled himself into a tight ball.

Lahassan knelt down beside him. In a mix of Hassani and Darija, he said, "We are in *my* territory." As he stood up above him, "Western Sahara is our land!"

The crowd around Lahassan cheered in accord.

Lahassan's men picked Azeddine up by the arms. The roar of the crowd subsided as Lahassan walked away. All Azeddine could make out was a faint glimmer of light in the distance, red and blue.

They untied his arms and told him to cup his hands as they poured water from one of their canteens. He gulped the water, trying not to let one drop escape. He looked up at the men then to the right at the lights. They forced him into a man-made hole.

The pit wasn't big enough for him to lie down in. The night was starting to get cold. He lay fetal position, trying to think about how he'd gotten this far. He breathed down his shirt trying to warm himself up but only shivered between breaths.

The serrated blade of the desert night began cutting through. He feared hypothermia would set in.

Half an hour later, he heard someone outside.

A young soldier appeared, Azeddine explained to me, "Like he come from ciel, un ange." Like an angel, he came out of nowhere and offered him an extra t-shirt, shoes, and a coat. The cadet wanted to trade information for warmth.

The boy was studying to be a nurse and someday a doctor. He wanted to know prescription details for various types of medicines. One of them, Azeddine explained, was quite dangerous and should only be used for those who are bleeding to death. Azeddine's mind flashed back to the young soldier with his leg blown off, the one he had tried to save.

The teenager dropped the gear down into Azeddine's pit. The tattered shoes had no laces; the shirt and jacket were too small but helped tremendously. This was Azeddine's first lesson in desert climate—its sweltering days and bone-chilling nights were one's main concern.

While he slept, he had the sensation he was floating through someone else's life. He recognized where he was. He saw the mantel back in his home; a silver frame encased a picture of his sister and younger brother. In another frame beside it was a photo of his mother and father. He tried to examine them closely but could only make out their silhouettes. A sound came from upstairs. A curtain blew behind him.

Someone was walking above the pit.

Azeddine jolted upright. Though he wasn't delusional, he felt like he'd been in a temporary coma.

As he climbed out of the pit, the sunlight warmed his face. It was dawn.

A wheelbarrow squeaked as it was being pushed to a nearby dirt pile. A Polisario guard took his arm as he emerged from the pit. Other captured detainees were laboring all around him. Azeddine noticed that many of them were Moroccan, some from Lebouirate. He couldn't believe it. There were so many. They looked like apathetic zombies, faces withered like the dehydrated grapes of the late winemaking season near Meknes. Another Polisario guard stood above them with a makeshift wire whip, puffing on a cigarette and watching his subjects as if they were ants digging tunnels. These tunnels were being dug into the side of a dry riverbed, possibly the tail end of the Saguia el-Hamra.

As the guard escorted Azeddine to join the workers, someone came around the side of the dirt pile carrying the end of a shovel missing its wooden handle and walked over to the guard.

With the end of the whip, the guard pointed him to another work pit.

"AHMED!"

Ahmed looked over his shoulder, then jumped into the pit.

Another guard marched over towards Azeddine and struck him in the chest, knocking him down.

"Le sable. The sand—"Azeddine's mouth had gone dry with the shock of seeing Ahmed again. The brute lashed and kicked him repeatedly.

"AHMED! AHMED! ALLAH! TU ES VIVANT!" Azeddine cried out. Ahmed was alive!

This time the guard kicked Azeddine in the stomach and blood splattered on the guard's pants and boots.

"AH-ha-MED," Azeddine panted. The guard kicked him even harder in the back of the head.

The dark chill of night enveloped him. He felt nothing. He looked at the formless photos on the mantel once again. His mother's soft voice beckoned. A gray mist came in with the breeze from behind. He tried going up the stairs, but couldn't turn away from the mantel.

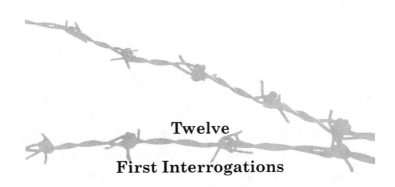

Twelve

First Interrogations

Almost all the POWs were tortured during the interrogation that followed their capture. One of the torturers most frequently mentioned is Ahmed Moulay Chrif Filali, also known as Aït Chrif, the former Deputy-Director of the Polisario Front security services, who now lives in Morocco. [One Moroccan POW named] Lieutenant Abdurrahman was captured in 1982. During his interrogation, he refused to give military information. He was set alight with kerosene by Ahmed Moulay Chrif Filali. When his torturers realized he was still alive, Adda Brahim Ould Hmim asked the guards who were present if one would volunteer to kill this Moroccan POW.

-The Conditions of Detentions of the Moroccan POWs Detained in Tindouf (Algeria). France Libertés, April 2003

FOR TWO days, Azeddine lay in something like a fox-hole somewhere along the dry path of the Saguia el-Hamra, given only rice and something akin to water. The liquid had a soapy odor and tasted of gasoline. None of that mattered though. Ahmed was alive. That was all that mattered.

He heard Lahassan talking just outside the hole. The brute laughed as he looked down into the pit and told Azeddine it was time to come out. Azeddine was still wearing the clothes that one of Lahassan's own soldiers had given him the previous night.

Lahassan pointed to a mound of dirt with a metal door on the front and told a guard to take Azeddine there.

"Hopefully you'll come out alive," he hissed in Azeddine's ear.

In the small dark room, Azeddine could barely see. A few Polisario officers sat on metal chairs. A man sitting between two others pulled out several documents, what looked like a newspaper, and a pen. A guard stood by the door.

The man sitting in the middle shifted himself upright and said something in Hassani to the guard, who immediately left. They switched to Darija.

"My name is Aït Chrif. I'm the Deputy-Director of Polisario Security Services," he said. "Please give us your last name, number, and rank."

"Benmansour. Azeddine. Medical Aspirant."

"What is your military number?"

"Medical staff are considered officers and are not given numbers in the Royal Moroccan Military."

"Are you not a doctor?"

"Yes. Is that all you would like to know, Shreef?" Azeddine used this title of utmost respect.

"You will answer all questions asked," the man said tersely.

His shirt collar seemed to tighten around his neck. He was a precisionist in his attire and make up: his hair was neatly combed, cut squarely on the sides, short on top. He was probably shaved three times a day, his eyebrows detailed, his hands manly but manicured. Even his green military uniform was wrinkle-free with the sleeves folded squarely to mid-forearm.

"I am a doctor, but now I do not know." Azeddine knew that giving him a hard time could get him another beating or thrown back into the hole. He tried remaining as calm as he could. "I completed my studies in general medicine in June of this year, 1979."

"What were you doing in Lebouirate?" Aït Chrif said coming off his chair a little.

"I don't know."

"C'est vrai," Azeddine said, shrugging his shoulders at me. It was the truth. "I never want problem with Polisario officers."

"What do you *mean*, you don't know?" Aït Chrif continued.

"It wasn't my choice to be there, Sir. I wasn't sure of my duties."

"You were to be a doctor! Right?"

"Yes, of course."

He looked at the ground, not wanting to look Aït Chrif in the face.

If Aït Chrif were to shoot him, this was the moment. Azeddine thought he had crossed some arbitrary line that determined whether he'd live or be tortured to death. He wanted to somehow relay to the man that even if he was a prisoner, he was still human and in no moral or humane way below him. Images of his dead patients covered in bloody sheets surfaced in his mind. If he were to say anything more, it might be a blatant leap into some fiery pit. "Your men killed my brothers!"

The expression on Aït Chrif's face did something Azeddine didn't predict. It calmed. He had managed to diffuse Chrif's inner bomb. After a pause, Chrif said, "We are here for one cause, Doctor. It was a display of our desire to be free from your king, Hassan II. The pain it causes us to think about remaining under that monarchy is much more painful than death."

Surprised at his response, Azeddine implored, "Let me go, along with my comrades—home, family. We'll tell you anything. We can give you nothing."

"Your freedom will be forsaken." Aït Chrif tapped his pen on the table, wanting to change the subject. "Are you familiar with any Royal Moroccan Military strategies or plans, Dr. Benmansour?"

Azeddine looked straight at him. He thought they'd already been through this. It could have been a formality. "No. I haven't been trained to do so. I can't even tell you which way is north."

Azeddine looked at me as if he were trying to rationalize his case to Chrif all over again. "In Casablanca, give me green military clothes, take to Lebouirate. Is all."

"Thank you for your time. You may leave." Chrif finalized something on his pad of paper.

"Can I have clean water? The water tastes like gasoline." Azeddine thought that now was as good a time as any to ask for his needs and to make sure they knew the conditions the captured Moroccans had to endure.

"I will talk to my officers." He raised his voice to the guard on the other side of the door. "Guard, help Dr. Benmansour out."

"Oh, Doctor, before you go," Chrif continued, "I thought you might like to see this." He held up a newspaper. His smile was highlighted in the dim light.

He motioned Azeddine to come and look at the headline. It was dated early August 1979 and was entitled *Saharawi Libre*. The headline read in Spanish, "Victory! Mauritania drops all claims to the Sahara!"

"You see we are *not* insurgents, Doctor. We have a vision. We do what it takes to win. This will be broadcast over our radios and connected to loudspeakers across the camps. We will continue on our planned path for liberation."

Azeddine wasn't surprised by the headline, due to recent political events. "Water, food, and shelter are the only things important to us right now," he continued, pressing for improvements on behalf of himself and the other prisoners.

"Doctor," Chrif replied scornfully, "you may be voicing your support for our cause over the loud speakers, spreading your newfound faith in us. People have a certain trust in doctors. Seer! Get out!"

Photo A (left):

Azeddine wearing his new Royal Moroccan Forces (FAR) military uniform before heading to Lebouirate.

Photo B (below):

Azeddine in his doctor's office in Polisario camps.

Photo C (right):

Azeddine changing camps after visiting with Dr. Ahmed.

Part Three: Transfigurations

In the name of the Saharawi people, and in pursuance of their will, the flag of the Saharawi Arab Democratic Republic has been raised over the land of Saguia el-Hamra and Rio de Oro. The birth of an African State with deep roots in the history of our people, with a civilization, which spread over the entire Maghreb, is so proclaimed.

- Proclamation of the Saharawi Arab Democratic Republic (SADR). February 27, 1976

Thirteen

Big Party

AZEDDINE DIDN'T know whether to believe the announcements over the loud speakers in the camps or not. The Polisario seemed to be attacking areas bordering the Sahara every day. Mauritania, who had dropped all claims to the Sahara, was now being given back the POWs the Polisario had captured near their border. It was just as Aït Chrif had predicted.

Azeddine wasn't allowed to talk to the Mauritanians still being held in the camps. Since both Morocco and Mauritania shared the French language, the Polisario wanted to limit any chances of organized revolts or riots. Azeddine knew the Polisario weren't inept. They'd studied somewhere, it seemed, the tactics of maintaining order in their camps. It took organization and a hierarchy of power, but most of all, it took fear.

Fall came and went without the changes of season that Azeddine had been used to in Fez. By mid-November, he would have seen heat-lightning spark across the dry, brown hillsides. Now in December, in the desert, the days were their shortest, the long winter nights colder than ever.

After his interrogation with Aït Chrif, he had been taken, along with over a hundred other prisoners, to a camp designated Douze Octobre. Ahmed had been placed somewhere else, Azeddine was not sure where. He figured Ahmed had been taken to Rabonée, the Polisario's administrative capital, over twenty miles away.

In the passing months, Azeddine was put to work. They were tunneling what would be used as a weapon and missile bunker in the side of the riverbed when Azeddine noticed someone jump into the pit.

"AHMED! In Allah's name, you're here! Praise to Allah!" Azeddine was overjoyed to see his friend.

Throwing his pick onto the ground, he put his arms around Ahmed. Both hugged, rocking each other from side to side. "I thought you were in Rabonée."

"They brought me back here for follow-up."

"Chrif is intimidating. I wanted to make him aware of what's going on over here and how we're being treated," Azeddine said as he held Ahmed's head.

"Be careful," Ahmed countered, looking over the edge of the ravine. "We know nothing. That's our story."

"You and I are only alive because we're doctors." Azeddine said, then asked in a hushed tone, "Is Omar alive?"

"He's alive. He was on the first shipment to the new camp, Dahkla."

"Why are they always naming these new camps, camps that we prisoners built, after cities in Western Sahara?"

"Azeddine, I haven't had the chance to tell you I'm sorry about that time you got beat for calling out my name. I couldn't react. They would use our friendship against us."

"I couldn't believe you were alive. I didn't even feel the beating," he lied. The incident had left bruises that ached for weeks.

"Khoya, my brother, stay safe," Ahmed said nervously after he spotted a guard approaching. He left Azeddine and hurried to an adjacent work-site.

Azeddine grabbed his pick, bent over, and dug at the ground outside the door of the bunker. He would miss Ahmed badly over the next several months.

In the spring of 2003, before I met Azeddine, I went on an excursion with a fellow teacher named David from the Ifrane School. He had a true passion for Africa. He had lived in Burkina Faso for nearly a decade. His French was like that of Western Africans. He planned a trip with our students into the desert, and I was to be a chaperone. Oddly enough, my main objective, as described by David, was to take care of only one student, named Youness, a pupil whose father was a renowned psychologist. Youness, however, was a little disturbed. He had been born while his father was still completing his degree, and the toddler became the center study of his practicum; Freud with a spoonful of Jung was the result, quite possibly an inhumane crime.

Following the five a.m. departure and the six-hour drive to the desert oasis of Merzouga, a local guide suited us each with a camel for a sunset stroll into the rolling golden dunes of the Sahara. I felt the dangerous allure of the place, a similar pull that Azeddine might have felt when he first laid his eyes on the desert's expansiveness.

The girls squealed as the camels spit and huffed while on our way into the Erg Chebi, the name given to this section of Moroccan desert. After three hours on camelback, we arrived at two gigantic black tents next to what was claimed as the biggest dune in the Sahara. I prayed there would be no sandstorms that night. Our guide cooked a vegetable tajine; we sat on traditional carpets and dined under les belles étoiles.

We inhaled the oily, vegetable dish in minutes. The students then went off. Before we knew it, we heard peals of laughter streaming down the massive dune. The students had managed to get their hands on a snowboard for the newly invented sport of dune surfing. Several came back with sand-burns on their elbows and hands. The student I was responsible for, Youness, had a sand burn across his cheek. He sat down on the carpet as if nothing had happened and didn't say a word. We cringed at his wound, but no one said anything.

Before dawn the next morning, I prepared to climb the massive dune ahead to witness the sunrise. I learned that Youness would be joining me. He was the only student who was willing to get up early. Somehow, we were on a shared wavelength.

Youness climbed the dune with as much endurance as a marathoner. He nearly beat me to the top. The sand burn on his cheek had healed a little during the night; maybe it had just looked worse in the firelight. The sun began peeking over the rolling horizon.

Running through the forest trails in Ifrane at 1700-

meters hadn't prepared me for this sort of challenge. We'd climb ten steps up, and then slide back five. Nearly half an hour later, we made it to the top, out of breath and drenched in sweat. The awe-inspiring sunrise gave way to a brilliant luster of red, orange and, finally, washed-out brown.

I never mentioned the sunrise in the desert to Azeddine because I didn't want to venerate a place where he had been a veteran of such hardship. Questions did linger in my mind: *Did he ever find splendor in the desiccation around him? Could beauty coexist with despair? Does daily strife and struggle mask other human needs?* I might ask him one day.

One numbing January night in 1981, Azeddine was startled awake. He was sleeping on his cot, wrapped in his blanket, when someone shone a flashlight inside the tent. The man ordered everyone to gather their belongings and to get into the back of the truck. Azeddine was in such a hurry that he nearly forgot his blanket in the process.

Along with several other truckloads of Moroccan prisoners, about 150 in all, they were transported like cattle for the slaughter. They were only going twenty-two miles, but the truck took over an hour to get to its destination. The prisoners shivered in what Azeddine swore was the coldest night he'd experienced.

The men were taken inside one of two huge black tents that would be their sleeping quarters. A megaphone blared that it was now two a.m., and they had two hours to sleep before the work shift began.

Azeddine, who found himself taken to a separate tent, slept on some pallets covered in cardboard. Several small stoves, the sort with single burners on top, lined the wall. He wrapped himself up in his blanket, scooped sand together to form a pillow, and slept.

He awoke to commotion outside. Hundreds of Moroccan prisoners were standing at attention. Marching before them stood a general holding a megaphone. Guards swung their whips, made of electrical wire, snapping them down on the prisoners.

"700 or 800 ensemble, together," Azeddine remembered.

A guard toting a wire whip struck randomly and only pointed where everyone should congregate.

Azeddine ran with his head covered. The general with the megaphone didn't see him, and he managed to get by without being lashed.

"On February twenty-seventh," the megaphone announced in Darija, "we will be hosting a celebration to mark the fifth-year anniversary of our Declaration of Independence."

Azeddine heard the lash of a whip nearby. He tried to squeeze himself between the crowd of fellow prisoners.

The man behind the megaphone jabbered on about the prowess of the Saharawi Arab Democratic Republic (SADR).

"Fellow representatives of the *free* world will be here to join us. We are going to make them remember and not forget our plight!" He pointed to the open wasteland of sand and said that in two months time, they were to build the SADR Plaza. Work shifts would begin at four a.m. and end at midnight. Lunch and dinner would be served on-site. Prisoners would be separated into designated battalions.

The guards collected names that had been scribbled on yellow paper. Azeddine tried to hear above the ruckus. Not wanting to look out of place, he walked over to a group already formed.

"Benmansour. Azeddine Benmansour?" The man with the megaphone was searching for him.

Azeddine covered himself and ran over to him.

The man with the megaphone told him it would be his duty to tend to the prisoners and to start with the one who'd just gotten his ear lashed off.

"Il n'y avait même pas une infirmerie," Azeddine said. There wasn't even an infirmary for over 800 people! The kitchen was to be where he treated the patients. When he asked about supplies: bandages, needles, clean water, and a butane stove, the man with the megaphone waved him off impatiently saying they'd get materials sooner or later.

The guard went on to tell him it was his job to make sure not a single prisoner missed a day in the next several weeks. The guard said his name was Hakim and, if he had any trouble, to come to him directly. Azeddine thought back to his friend Hakim, the decapitated marksman with the rare green eyes who he'd left lying in the dust of Lebouirate. He came out of his momentary reflection to say, "Bien sûr, Sidi Hakim."

The prisoners toiled from before daybreak until midnight.

They were instructed to erect a stage, bury flagpoles, and construct a service kitchen and restrooms. Nineteen hours a day, day after day, prisoners heaved bricks, dug pits, and carted sand.

Azeddine worked as the sole physician on site but

also labored alongside the others during the hottest part of the day. He sacrificed a piece of his blanket to use as a turban to protect his head from the intensity of the sun, then left it on at night to keep the heat from escaping. Once he had gotten used to the gnawing lice, it was foolproof.

Breakfast was never served at four a.m. It wasn't until noon, when they got called in groups of ten. Each prisoner would squat around a halved gas barrel that was used as a central serving dish. The prisoners weren't given water to wash their hands, and were only allotted ten minutes to shovel fistfuls of rice and beans into their mouth.

On numerous occasions, guards withheld lunch, making the captives wait until midnight to eat. Azeddine's stomach cramped. He could only imagine what the others must have felt.

Abstaining from food and drink was usually a sacred practice most often done during the holy month of Ramadan. Each evening means a breaking of the fast, called Ftour, that families use as a time to celebrate after another day of fasting for Allah. It is a time of cleansing, holiness, and even meditation. The forced starvation by the Polisario upon the prisoners, however, was anything but holy. It was persecution.

Azeddine explained that the guards didn't differentiate between those they beat, those they starved, or those they treated decently from time to time. Some days the guards and officers were in a good mood. Other days, everyone would feel their wrath.

"They like Sahara storms," Azeddine related. The guards' tempers were radical and unpredictable. He couldn't bear to watch his fellow Moroccans undergo so much suffering, but nothing he could do would alleviate their torture. In the Polisario's eyes, Azeddine wasn't a doctor treating humans, but a veterinarian treating mules.

Ten days later, three prisoners approached him. They begged him to write a prescription giving them each a day off. He couldn't, not after what Hakim had told him.

He noticed how sunken and bloodshot their eyes were so he gave them a quick check-up.

"I cannot give days," Azeddine explained. "Or else, Hakim will not take my diagnoses seriously."

"Allah yrhm el walidin!" May God bless your parents, they begged of him.

The next day he went to talk to Hakim and told him these young prisoners had severe eye problems. If they weren't treated, they could go blind.

During their consultation with Azeddine, they described their sleeping quarters. "C'était déguelasse, vraiment déguelasse." It was absolutely revolting.

Inside their tent, buckets overflowed with urine and excrement. By two in the morning, the stench was so overwhelming that they would start puking in unison. Some of them had even tried to cover the buckets with plastic bags, but it was no barrier against the smell—a living hell.

He thought about approaching Hakim. "J'avais peur—I scared," Azeddine said outloud. "But, I know what I must do.

The three young men were thankful when Hakim allowed them a day of respite. They shook Azeddine's hand and walked away patting their hands over their hearts in the usual Moroccan manner. This was a sign of respect, but it made Azeddine feel even more helpless.

Night after night, Azeddine would hear masses of his comrades coughing, puking, and moaning in their tents. Emaciated after three weeks of severe physical labor and torment, the prisoners walked with heavy steps and heavier hearts. Conditions never improved. Azeddine, everyone, was beyond fatigued. His allotted time to consult with patients was from midnight to one a.m. This left him three hours to sleep.

During two of those nights, he watched through a hole in his tent as a guard tortured a Saharawi man. The man spoke Darija and Hassani. He was led with a paper bag over his head and thrown into a deep sandy crevasse. When they took the paper bag off, they placed a truck-tire over his head onto his shoulders. When he needed to use the bathroom, the guard took him out of the hole, put the paper bag over his head, and escorted him a hundred meters away.

Azeddine never saw the tortured man again.

About three days later, a prisoner ran up to Azeddine, muttering something about Mohammed's eye. Azeddine ran to where everyone was gathered. Guards and prisoners huddled together.

Mohammed was bent over in the sand covering his face. Hakim arrived, hollering at everyone to get back to work. The guards started shoving people away but, surprisingly, didn't swing their whips.

Hakim demanded to know what had happened. Mohammed rocked backed and forth spitting up blood. Azeddine put his hand on Mohammed's shoulder and asked if he could look. Mohammed's eye hung out of its socket. It had a milky-white film over it and his pupil wouldn't dilate. Blood ran down his cheek.

Mohammed was forty-five, captured while doing civilian labor near the Sahara border. Once Mohammed was able to walk, Hakim ordered Azeddine to take him back to the tent.

Even if he were able to put the eye back in, it would be useless. Azeddine didn't have the tools to operate. He told Hakim that Mohammed needed to be transported to Rabonée, the main camp where Ahmed was being held. Knowing it was the only place that could treat him, Hakim agreed. That night, Mohammed was taken to the Polisario Military Hospital in Raboneé. Azeddine hoped he could go along to see Ahmed.

Over the next few days, the tension at the camp mounted. The guards didn't beat or whip anyone. But soon after, they were back to their old habits of striking prisoners at random.

Two more weeks had passed when one of the prisoners was too sick to come out of the tent to see Azeddine in the infirmary. It was the first time Azeddine was allowed inside the other prisoners' tent. The odor assaulted his nostrils. The man lay in a far corner, holding his stomach. Azeddine knelt down and took his temperature; it was 105 degrees. After a couple of minutes, he knew the man, who he learned was named Abdelghani, was suffering from acute peritonitis. Something in his abdomen was hard to the touch and caused him a great deal of pain, even when the area was gently pressed. It would not be surprising if his appendix had ruptured during a beating. He stood up and walked over to Hakim.

Hakim refused to transport the sick prisoner to Rabonée. Azeddine glared at him, telling him the young man's condition was critical, and he would most likely die by the next day if not transported immediately.

Hakim informed him that the director of security was coming to the camp that night; there were no vehicles to transport the sick prisoner.

Azeddine and three others carried Abdelghani on his cot to Hakim's door; he continued to wail in agony. All they could do was cover him with the few blankets they had. Somehow, he was transported to Rabonée that night. A visiting Cuban doctor operated on him, and he came through and survived. The prisoner returned to the camp some weeks later and embraced Azeddine, kissing him on both cheeks. He even gave Azeddine a can of tuna—a true gift indeed.

The plaza was completed three days before the announced Independence Day Celebration. That day, the prisoners were all well fed, rested, and permitted to shower and shave. On the day of the party, they weren't allowed to engage in the festivities, so they were transported back to their camp at the Douze Octobre and closely monitored. They were told to stay on their cots and keep their talking to a minimum, as journalists and delegates wandered freely around the camp. The SADR flag flapped indignantly beside the other flags of the visiting representatives.

While lying on his cot, Azeddine noticed some people peeking at him. According to the information that these delegates were given, the Moroccan prisoners were being treated fairly. The countries invited to the event were those that recognized the SADR as an independent governing body, and they had no reason to disbelieve the fabricated reports from Polisario headquarters.

It was agreed that the POWs would be held only temporarily. They were political pawns caught in the middle. *Who would make the next move? Which government would outdo the other? What would the muffled sounds and flickering lights of his captor's victory party do for those who labored under torturous conditions?*

After the commemoration, the prisoners were taken back to the plaza. They worked there for a few more weeks, tearing down the stage and cleaning up the entire site. Azeddine walked by a bottle buried in the sand. He picked it up and poured out the contents. The red pool dissipated into the thick sand. The now flagless poles once waved the SADR flag proudly. A flag displaying the colors of Islam.

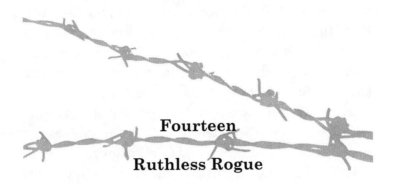

Fourteen

Ruthless Rogue

Early and mid 1980s

ONCE THE water was boiling, Azeddine sterilized any needles and other tools in the pot. Mehdi flinched from the prick of the needle, then reclined in the chair as his blood filled the bag. "Emiks emik." Take it easy. Azeddine often used Berber, some of the prisoner's native language, in an attempt to make them feel comfortable.

Azeddine heard someone outside. "Shkoon?"

Lemam, a guard no one liked, entered. In his nonchalant way, he informed Azeddine to be in the infirmary the next morning, since he was being shipped to the École Douze Octobre, a school called the Twelfth of October.

Azeddine continued cleaning the equipment, and the procedure with Mehdi was almost finished.

The next day, he waited until twelve-thirty for a guard

to accompany him to the school. He had had to forsake his portion of mushy rice at lunchtime for the occasion. The guards moved at their own leisurely pace.

Upon arrival at the school, the guard instructed him to wait in the hall. Sometime later, he returned, showing Azeddine to a comfortable room with plush couches, a small kitchen, and a large table in the center with hand-carved wooden chairs. At the table was a man Azeddine had only heard of via rumors.

It was Sidi Ahmed El Batal, the recently appointed head officer of Polisario military security. Supposedly, he was also said to be the despot heading Camp X, the infamous torture camp.

Batal sat back as he dined. Servants were there to tend to his needs. One came in carrying more soup.

"He have couscous, soup, and the best vegetables!" Azeddine chimed. The soup was an especially filling type called harira.

Batal told him that he had arrived too late to join him for lunch. Azeddine knew that Batal would never ask such a lowly spoil of war to share a table with him.

Sidi Ahmed El Batal had been moved up in rank to Directeur de la Sécurité Militaire, giving him complete control over the camps. When representatives of international organizations and committees wanted to speak to the person in charge, it was Batal they went to see.

Batal had started a plague of severe torturing across the camps in an effort to extract all the military information he could out of the prisoners. If a prisoner dared escape, he would be at the mercy of this man.

Sidi Ahmed El Batal was a nickname given to him

by the Spanish, signifying "one who loves battle." He was known to bind prisoners like animals. Following, he would burn the flesh of their backs to the second or third degree in order to make them talk. If that didn't work, he hung them upside-down, naked, while guards repeatedly kicked their head, eventually knocking them unconscious or, worse, killing them.

Batal asked Azeddine if he knew why he had been brought there. He did not. Batal seemed like a man who enjoyed talking for the sake of hearing himself abase others—his subjects.

He slurped the last of his soup and told Azeddine, "You will be teaching a new group of nursing students."

"Qu'est-ce que je pouvais faire?" Azeddine repeated to me. "What could I do?"

He was busier than ever, now that they were bringing in more prisoners as well as their own injured, not to mention being the only doctor in the camp; he was up to his ears in responsibility.

"I tell him I can not teach in Hassani and my Spanish no good."

Batal then told Azeddine he would have to teach the course in Fus'ha, Classical Arabic.

When Azeddine was growing up, his primary and secondary education was mainly conducted in French. At the university level, most courses were also taught in French. Courses taught in Fus'ha included Philosophy, Theology, Literature, and Islamic Law. His knowledge of French was by far superior to his skills in Classical Arabic. He wouldn't be able to express concepts or use correct medical terminology if he had to teach in Fus'ha. Of course he spoke Darija, but it's a spoken language used at home and on the street, never in formal education.

Batal pointed to a box resting on some cushions. It contained medical supplies, a few books, a blank pad of paper, and two unsharpened pencils. He recognized the books immediately. They were Ahmed's. He looked over at Batal who finished rolling a couscous ball and popped it into his mouth. He told Azeddine he had ten days to put the class together. The class would be ongoing for several months.

There was no getting out of it. No matter how much he debated, he would have to acquiesce to Batal's whims. Two servants entered and cleared away the rest of the dishes that lay before him.

Azeddine prepared the course to the best of his ability. He jotted down his notes in French and decided that when he was in front of the class lecturing, he'd be able to relay it in Fus'ha. It just didn't sound right though. Fus'ha was too formal. He felt as if he were back in the Middle Ages delivering a speech before the king.

He couldn't stand the fact that he was abetting Batal, a Moroccan himself who was subjecting his own people to such abject conditions for a cause they defied.

"Il a fait une guerre dans sa propre ville natale!" Azeddine said. Batal had raided his own village.

Ten days later, Azeddine returned to the school. This time a pilot named Mustapha was ordered to go with him. Mustapha spoke English quite well. He had even been to the United States to receive training as a fighter pilot.

"Why are you going to see Batal?" Azeddine asked him.

"Batal wants to learn English so he can steal more money from the NGOs and non-profit organizations," Mustapha retorted.

Mustapha had three days to conjure up a course for Batal and was to focus on "useful political phrases."

Ten students stared as Azeddine walked to the front of the classroom. A new chalkboard hung on the wall. A strange man stood beside it. He had dark skin and sparkling white teeth. He introduced himself as Rashid, a Mauritanian who spoke both Classical Arabic and French. He would be the translator.

"I have translator. I'm very important person," Azeddine joked to me, straightening his sweater. "Professor Azeddine."

He wondered why this Mauritanian was still here. After all, they had been freed some years ago.

Rashid was something novel for Azeddine, a fresh new face outside the camp. Three days a week, he knew Rashid would be waiting beside the chalkboard.

He started the first day with a lesson in anatomy. Rashid had difficulty translating the bodily organs so the next day, he had a medical dictionary with him.

"Students knows nothing, même pas biologie." The people sitting before him, these so-called nursing students, didn't even know the basics of high-school biology.

After a month, Azeddine frequented the school less, only when the guards of the school remembered to pick him up. Eventually, the more loquacious Omar El Hadrami replaced Batal (a move by Algeria's military intelligence). Hadrami had established connections with the international community and had already orchestrated several negotiations between France and Algeria.

Little did the Polisario know at that time that Hadrami would later attempt a coup inside the Polisario camps that would shake the Polisario structure for nearly a decade. After Hadrami's subsequent pardon and release from a Saharawi prison by Polisario military leaders, he was given the post of representative to Washington, D.C. Shortly thereafter, however, on a return trip from the United States' capitol, Hadrami defected back to Morocco where King Hassan II welcomed him with open arms, never bringing him to trial for his crimes against humanity.

Azeddine was glad he no longer had to prepare for the students, but he missed seeing Rashid, who had become a friend over the past weeks.

Batal had been reassigned to carry out attacks near the Sahara Border.

"He has great gift for war, evil gift."

Throughout the 1980s, Morocco carried through with its plans to build an immense barrier of sand dubbed the "Berm" along its border in Western Sahara. At the Berm's completion, it would be nearly half the size of the Great Wall of China. Strategically positioned, it was planted with mines and patrolled by the Royal Armed Forces (FAR) ready to counterattack any raids made by the Polisario.

By the mid-1980s, the first parts of the wall were complete. Its first segments were built around the phosphate-rich cities of Boucra and Smara. The Polisario knew of Morocco's plans to build the wall and this infuriated them to no end.

Batal's new job was to raise the number of Polisario attacks in order to destroy Morocco's newly constructed fortification. "Two grandes batailles. Marocains, Polisario and Algériens die," Azeddine said sadly. The first major battle occurred in Boucra in September 1982. The next was in Smara, one year later. "Allah come to us in Smara in September of 1983."

Morocco had new fighter jets, Gazelle Helicopters, dubbed the "fire birds of Allah." This bold move answered many Moroccans' prayers. *Was this how it would all end?* Maybe Morocco would slowly start taking the areas around the wall, eventually seizing the entire border and rescuing the prisoners.

Azeddine feared this incident would leave Batal more bloodthirsty than ever and seeking vengeance on the prisoners.

A few weeks later, the Moroccan POWs found out Batal had been badly injured in an explosion. He hadn't lost a leg or even an arm. It was rumored, however, that he had been blinded. Cuban and Russian doctors did all they could but nothing brought back his sight. He was stripped of his military title and made an honorary Minister of Information. He would live on, perhaps in atonement for all the crimes against his own people.

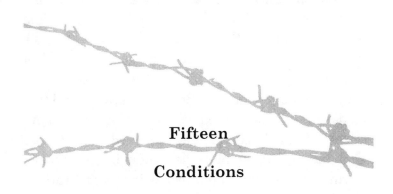

Fifteen

Conditions

The fact that several non-governmental organizations have decided to stop backing the Polisario mercenaries provides crystal-clear evidence to the end of their theses and lies.... [We stand] ready to provide governmental and non-governmental organizations cogent proofs on Polisario's human rights breaches and [the] embezzlement of humanitarian aid.

- Statement by *ASVIPO, Association of Victims of Human Rights Violations in Polisario Prisons*

Spring 2002

FROM A tiny perch in my Peace Corps village, I could see fresh snow on the trail leading to the top of Mount Toubkal, the highest peak in North Africa. Azeddine often asked me about my time there. My appointed village was three hours away from the well-visited town of Setti-Fatima down below.

Hikers often passed by as they walked the popular route to Mount Toubkal and east to Imlil. Brahim would usually invite them inside. If they spoke English, I could translate some of their basic questions: "What do you do in the village? Where do you work? How many kids do you have?" Brahim answered politely, but deep inside, he wanted help. I knew he would have welcomed any donations; much needed funds to buy vegetables, bread, or oil. I also knew he appreciated me, an environmental volunteer, being there. Truth be told, we both knew I couldn't teach the villagers how to better irrigate or farm their steep mountainside. Maybe I could get them money, a grant, to help install toilets or proper irrigation canals.

I spent most of those days outside playing with the Berber mountain kids, their cheeks red from the altitude. Those used to tourists voiced their need much more blatantly. From the corner of their mud houses, they'd chant, "Donnez-moi un stylo." Give me a pen. If that didn't work, then, "Donnez-moi un bonbon." Give me some candy. And, if all else failed, it came to a monetary request just to see what they *might* get before hurrying off. "Donnez-moi un dirham." Give me a dirham.

Brahim offered visitors hot mint tea with a dash of sheeba, or absinthe. Illegal in the United States and parts of Europe due to its toxicity, it is widely used in Morocco and said to keep you warm during the winter months. Moroccans share a laugh by calling their sweet tea "Whiskey Morocain." With absinthe, I wondered if they knew how close it truly was.

Tourists often partook of the snack and continued

with the 4,167-meter (13,671 ft.) peak of Mount Toubkal on their minds—easily viewable from places such as Marrakesh on clear days. In my mind, the village needed something to offer tourists besides hospitality. They might form a cooperative and use their skills to sell wares to passersby.

After Peace Corps, I spent some time in Ifrane, the Swiss-like mountain village that looks more like Europe than Africa. The winter is as glorious as the fall. It is Morocco's only town that receives as much heavy snow as the country's high mountain peaks.

Azeddine reminisced about his childhood visits to Ifrane with his family and seeing all the vacationing French tourists. In the desert, though, it was a different kind of cold. He explained that during his imprisonment, he had felt like the impoverished children in the mountains: hungry and cold.

In my dreams or while daydreaming, I'm not sure, I walked along the snowbound trails inside the forest. The branches of cedars were weighed down with mounds of snow. I came up to a wide-open space where blood had stained the white, like drips from a cherry Popsicle.

A bloody tooth with frozen roots lay beside a tree that had dropped bits of frozen lichen over the ground. I wondered which of the forest dwellers, wild dogs, boars, monkeys, or jackals had gotten into a scuffle. *Which animal survived? Which retreated?* Undoubtedly, the blood would stain the ground until the winter came to pass.

Late 1980s to early 1990s

Azeddine was stationed in Douze Octobre for many years, while Ahmed worked to the northwest, in Rabonée. Throughout the years, the prisoner count grew from the upper-hundreds into the thousands. New camps were constructed, and prisoners slaved on. Life inside the camps didn't improve for anyone until non-governmental organizations (NGOs) started paying attention. When the UN declared a ceasefire, to which Morocco and the Polisario half-heartedly agreed in 1991, conditions in the camps gradually got better.

Azeddine was part of a work group that had installed a water reservoir for the prisoners in his camp. But what bothered him most was the Polisario's decision not to cover it, leaving the well open to the elements. Sand from weeklong Chergui or Sirocco sandstorms contaminated the entire supply. This led to increased sickness, mainly diarrhea, making Azeddine's job all the more difficult. The tank often leaked, and the prisoners had to wait days for a cistern truck to arrive, bringing equally contaminated quantities of non-potable water for them to drink. If there was a way to boil the water, they would. Azeddine and the other prisoners often went one or two days without a single drop. Plus, they were only allowed to drink once the Saharawi refugees got their fill.

Severe cases of dysentery plagued the camp, made worse since the prisoners weren't allowed to leave their tents at night. Forty or fifty men slept side by side and had to relieve themselves inside the tents too.

Azeddine made excuses to the guards so he could

sleep in the kitchen tent, the infirmary, as far away from the malodorous tents as possible. This didn't keep him from getting sick, but it meant that he could run out to the field if needed.

He couldn't keep sickness from spreading or contamination to a minimum.

One of the most important jobs of a physician is to maintain a sanitary work area. It was nearly impossible for him to hold to the high standards of his profession in the Polisario camps, especially in the new infirmary the Polisario decided to construct: a hole dug in the ground and encased in tin.

"On avait des scorpions, des mouches, et des araignées," Azeddine said as he showed me the size of the scorpions, flies, and spiders that would frequent the underground infirmary.

Being a prisoner himself, and the camp doctor, he had more duties to fulfill than he had time. During the early mornings, an hour or so before the sun came up, he'd rise before everyone else, and administer any necessary medications to the prisoners. One new prisoner had severe diabetes and had to have a ready supply of insulin. Azeddine reflected on the steady hands of Nurse Omar, who had been placed in Camp Dahkla. He could have used his help now.

Many times, the rations of medications ran out. He could do nothing but wait until the new allocations arrived. For the diabetic patient, he kept as much insulin as the Polisario doctors at Rabonée would give him. He stored it in a small butane-powered refrigerator at the camp director's office.

The prisoners were busy building new administration facilities for the Polisario. Every day, each prisoner he saw begged him for some excuse not to work. They would say, "Praise be to Allah and your family, Sidi Azeddine."

Every prescription that called for a prisoner not to work meant a Polisario guard interrogating the doctor who prescribed it. Sympathetic prescriptions had to be reserved for the direst cases.

One prisoner named Hamid was allowed a day's rest due to a hernia. When he was denied an operation in Rabonée, he hid beneath a truck in hopes of getting there clandestinely. With the afternoon heat, Hamid fell asleep, only to wake up with the weight of the moving truck crushing him. He was finally rushed to the Polisario Military Hospital in Rabonée.

Azeddine was questioned about the incident by the head guard of the camp.

"They cover it up. They no want NGOs to ask why." Azeddine's English was becoming better than my French. The Polisario had been thriving on outside assistance, aid that never reached the prisoners.

"I go school pendant huit ans, for eight years." He got up and walked over to the window. "They never correct with us. Polisario guard dogs treated better."

Azeddine looked away from the window. "Conditions only better for Polisario. We eat nothing. NGOs give good rice. We do work. We teach French. We see *no* money, *no* clothes, *no* food!" He began pacing around the living room. "We go to toilet in bucket."

Every two weeks, individual prisoners were given two gallons of water to shower. Azeddine used it sparingly.

He put it in a kettle so he could pour it over himself and shower in moderation. In January or February, he'd heat it on a butane stove to have warm water. With what was left, he washed his undergarments. The worst part was using *Tide,* the laundry detergent, or as Azeddine pronounced it, "Teed." "Regarde, je suis chauve à cause de ça," he said as he motioned me to rub my hand over his bald scalp. The top of his head was eternally blemished and irritated because of the stuff.

In the early years of his imprisonment, breakfast was nonexistent. By the latter 1980s, however, each prisoner was given a pouch of powdered milk and, if lucky, leftover rice from the night before. The Saharawi refugees ate in their school cafeterias or in their tents. Azeddine ate outside alongside his comrades with sand blowing in their faces and food. It was hard not to starve.

Ten years of his captivity passed with hardly any fruit, vegetables, or meat for Azeddine or the other prisoners. They subsisted on rice, vermicelli, and beans. On rare occasions, they'd get their hands on cans of sardines long expired. Unfortunately, this windfall did more harm than good, as prisoners would become sick, losing vital energy and precious fluids.

When there were food shortages, prisoners were given a flour-water mixture in order to survive: one gallon to every ten men. To watch them endure the extreme physical exertion was hard enough, but witnessing his comrades suffer malnourishment was beyond what the average psyche could bear.

By the end of 1987 and throughout 1988, the Spanish

government sent in an NGO to help the Polisario and the prisoners. In some of the bigger camps, they supplied materials necessary to build dome-like shelters resembling igloos. "Igloo en désert. Without snow," Azeddine jested.

These new cells proved better than the underground barracks and tattered tents. They withstood sandstorms and rain, stayed cool in the summer and warm in the winter. Now, instead of forty to fifty men cramped inside a massive tent, only two or three shared the same sleeping space. Azeddine noticed tension in the camp subside and the overall morale of the prisoners increase.

Despite such improvements, he was still preoccupied. At night, he lay awake thinking about his family. His dreams now held the pictures of his past life. Although bleary and distant in his visions, he was satisfied in knowing they were still with him. He pictured his father, almost twelve years older than when he had last seen him. His father had a magical way of looking young and was still crafting furniture, a trade that had been passed down from his grandfather.

Azeddine felt like praying, thankful he was still alive. He often fell asleep wondering what his life would have been like had he not been captured. *Would he have his own medical practice? Be married to a wonderful woman? Be a father?*

What sights do I see?
Sand, rain, day's eve.
The swirling mix of colors.
What sights shall I see?

Azeddine awoke in the early dark hours. Over the years, the Polisario had been given generous amounts of resources intended for the Moroccan prisoners. These contributing NGOs and organizations truly believed the Polisario were distributing these resources to the prisoners. The world is so easily fooled. Maybe they had heard the prisoners' cries across the desert.

What sights shall we see?
The swirling mix of colors,
reflected in this silent war.

Sixteen

An Unveiling

Some of the POWs confided their bitterness to us when, years later, US POWs captured during the second Iraqi war were shown on TV and those images triggered an international outcry that simply never existed for them [Moroccan POWs]. In fact, right into the eighties, the Moroccan POWs would not only be used by the Polisario Front for the propaganda targeting the media, but also to create the illusion that they were being well treated…. They were prepared in advance so as to give a good image of their detention and exposed "like animals in a zoo," to use the words of one of the POWs.

- The Conditions of the Moroccan POWs Detained in Tindouf (Algeria), France Libertés, April 2003

Early to mid 1990s

AZEDDINE WAS leery when the face of good fortune smiled upon him and the others. The Polisario never did anything to improve the conditions or treatment of the prisoners unless it benefited them.

In the Neuf Juin camp, where Azeddine had now been placed, there was talk of a visit by the International Red Cross. The prisoners were hopeful, but they were still forced to work hard.

They were forced to abnegate all forms of sports and exercise after one prisoner had used it to his advantage. The guards had allowed one prisoner, a pilot, to exercise, and they found it amusing that he'd work forced labor from sun-up to midnight and still ask if he could jog around the compound. Little did they recognize that he was training for the run of his life—a run that would ultimately bring freedom.

Following the Polisario's manhunt for the pilot, they only found a jeep with no gas and two empty canteens lying in the sand. The pilot had run the half-marathon distance, reaching the border near an unfinished section of the sand wall, where Moroccan military patrolmen discovered him en route. Somehow, the pilot knew exactly what to do, how to do it, and where to go. From there, he had been taken for questioning and released home to his family in Marrakesh.

Azeddine was still getting used to Neuf Juin. It was more crowded than Douze Octobre, but the infirmary was better. He had managed to spend a few days with Ahmed, who was also in transition to another camp.

Standing outside, washing his hands with cold water, he looked up and saw a guard give Ahmed a soccer ball and say "Yallah!" Let's go!

Ahmed didn't ask questions. He kicked the ball to another prisoner, who started bouncing it off his knees.

Soon, many of the onlookers joined. They found rocks to use as imitation goal posts on their surrogate field, and the game was on.

Prisoners came out of their huts, squinting in the mid-morning sun in disbelief. Soon, the entire camp was on the dirt field, kicking the ball to whoever was in its path.

Azeddine watched Ahmed run. He was limber. From a distance, they looked like carefree school children. Before long, Azeddine took off his white lab coat and began jogging around the field, not caring whether he kicked the ball or not.

Ahmed passed him the ball. He kicked it to Latif, who displayed fancy footwork but missed the goal. They all threw their hands in the air and cheered anyway.

Azeddine wanted to run as fast as he could. He wanted to run because he hadn't in so long, and it felt good. He got a stitch in his side, but didn't care because he hadn't felt this free in over a decade.

Not ten minutes had passed when a white Land Rover with tinted windows pulled up inside the camp. Two people got out and watched them on the field. The driver rolled down his window to snap a few pictures with his professional-looking camera.

"Who is—?" Azeddine asked, as if he and I had been transported back and were now standing on the field with the others. "Who are these people?"

The prisoners stopped in unison, staring at the Land Rover. The visitors stayed, snapping photos for a few more minutes and then drove off.

Once they were gone, a Polisario guard came from the sidelines, struck Latif in the head, and confiscated the ball. Azeddine and the others were stunned as the guard walked off, realizing they had just been duped for a media ploy.

Ahmed picked up a round rock and started kicking it. The game was back in session.

The same guard came back out of his shack. He ran up to Ahmed, tripped him, and kicked him in the stomach. He grabbed the rock and flung it with all his might, aiming near the ground at Ahmed's head.

Ahmed lay on the ground unmoving as guards chased the other prisoners off the field.

Ahmed got up, blood dripping down his mouth and chin. He wiped his face with his shirt. Over the cacophony, Azeddine signaled for him to get to the infirmary.

They went inside. Azeddine felt a surge of blood course through his body. He wanted to do it again, to feel that same freedom. He wondered if Ahmed felt the same way.

From then on, Azeddine secretly exercised inside the infirmary for twenty or thirty minutes, two times a week. After the guards had eaten lunch in the early afternoon, they'd take an hour siesta before changing shifts. During that hour, Azeddine pretended he had work to do in the infirmary. Instead, he'd do push-ups, jumping jacks, or run in place. He thought of anything he could do within the confines of the small space.

The guards must have rethought their strategy. The next day the prisoners were forewarned they'd be having visitors. This meant they would be spending the morning cleaning up the camp in assigned work groups.

That afternoon, they were all given two gallons of water to shower with and dull razors to share. They stood in line as Latif, once a barber and now a proven soccer player, came by with scissors, trimming their overgrowth. After each one was shaved, the razors were collected and distributed to the next in line.

Azeddine had been able to shave regularly. He had convinced the Polisario medical officer on site that it was best if he were clean-shaven. He knew their doctor wouldn't object since Azeddine treated Polisario members as well.

Tide was the detergent of choice in the camps. It was used for just about anything: from shampoo to shaving cream, dish soap to engine-grease remover. After their showers, they were given decent second-hand clothes to wear. Azeddine's green sweatshirt had "Gucci" written in big yellow letters across the chest. It was comfortable and didn't smell too bad, either.

"The pullover," he said happily. "I take it to infirmary after!"

The guards told the prisoners to go to bed early.

One hour before midnight, Azeddine peered out from behind the officers' hut. It had been recently built and still needed a coat of paint. Fresh white paint would be used on the rounded caps of the structure that would serve two main purposes: to reflect the sun's rays and to keep scorpions at bay; they wouldn't risk making themselves visible to prey.

He heard a rumbling of vehicles, then spotted three Land Rovers, like the one he had seen when they were playing soccer.

He could partially make out who they were from the glare of the trucks' lights. One black man wore dark pants and a brown cap. A white woman in her mid-forties, wearing shiny boots and a pocket-laden vest, was talking with him. Another portly man climbed out from behind the passenger's side. He wore a dark shirt and had a short beard. He put his hands on his hips and leaned back, stretching to the sky. He looked around and then began chatting with the other two.

Azeddine guessed they were journalists or part of the Red Cross. Ahmed, who was sharing the officers' quarters with Azeddine, confirmed there was a new structure being built in Rabonée, a hotel of sorts for visiting organizations.

He and Ahmed lay on their cots pondering the sheer lies the guard would feed these outsiders.

They were whispering to each other when they heard feet approaching.

"You'll be able to see their day-to-day life here. They're fine. You'll understand why they don't want to go back to their homes," a Polisario guard was telling these visitors in French as he gave them a tour of the camp.

The guard entered the domed-structure holding a flashlight above his head and scanning around Azeddine and Ahmed's bunk. He went to Azeddine, saying a journalist wanted to interview one of the physicians.

Why hadn't they asked Ahmed? Maybe it was because he had been working at the hospital in Rabonée and hadn't been in the outlying camps as much. Azeddine walked out of the spherical hut. The guard grabbed him by the back of his shirt and warned him he had better be "careful in what you say."

The journalist shook Azeddine's hand and said he was from French News Channel Three. He was the bearded man Azeddine had seen while they were playing soccer. The reporter shook his hand for an unusually long time, as if checking for the pains of his labor.

The reporter said in French, "I'd like to ask you some questions. Can we go to the infirmary?"

The guard stayed close behind them. The infirmary was only twenty-five yards away. The guard shone his flashlight inside which cast their shadows onto the bare cinder-block walls. Azeddine wished he could have taken the man to a proper medical facility, but he also wanted the man to see the reality of their situation. He noticed the record books and typewriter were missing, along with the signs showing how a patient should prepare to give blood. One sign remained, however, concealed behind his white lab coat that was hanging on the wall.

Azeddine casually went over, took his lab coat off the hook, shook it, and put it on, pretending to be cold. The guard didn't catch on to Azeddine's ruse. Azeddine and the journalist sat down in the infirmary's two rusty folding chairs with old t-shirts taped on for padding. He positioned his chair so the French journalist was facing the sign. The guard stood by the door.

"Vous allez bien?" Are you fine?

I'm being held captive. I'm hungry, tired, and mentally eroded, he wanted to say on first impulse, but said, "Oui. Bien sûr." Yes, of course. He coughed, looking up at the sign.

"Donc," the reporter continued. "My name is Mathew, and I just have a few questions to ask. First, what is your position on the Sahara Question?"

With the guard standing there, Azeddine knew he had to monitor his answers. "The Sahara Question?" he repeated to me, still pondering its meaning.

"If you are referring to the situation here," he responded to Mathew, "I simply hope a peaceful and prompt solution is found."

The journalist shook his head. Azeddine's heart raced.

"Can I ask you, why Doctor, why don't you and the prisoners want to go home? Is it that much better for you here, or is it that you believe the Saharawi people deserve to have their land?"

What was this man trying to do? Get him beaten? Was he that gullible? The guard stared intently.

Then, another soldier called the guard. The journalist signaled that he'd be all right, and the guard left abruptly.

Once the guard was out of hearing distance, Azeddine scooted forward, closer to the reporter. He looked back at the door and whispered, not caring if he was being presumptuous, "You cannot ask me these types of questions. I can't answer you honestly. The guard— I'll be punished, tortured." Azeddine tried to keep his voice down. "We are imprisoned against our will. These aren't my normal clothes," as he tugged at his sweatshirt. "We are overworked, not given rest, and many are malnourished. Our circumstances are deplorable. Prisoners are forced to give blood to aid the fighting Saharawi refugees and the Polisario." Azeddine pointed to where his lab coat had been hanging.

The sign was in French. The journalist read it aloud. It said, "After giving blood you are entitled to a snack, a glass of milk, and a day of rest."

"This is against everything signed in Geneva."

The journalist's mouth was agape. He skimmed over the sign, crossed out his entire page of notes and stood up.

The guard returned, checking the office. He noticed the exposed poster behind Azeddine. The reporter said he had all the information he needed and left. The guard glared at Azeddine, then followed the reporter.

The next day, Azeddine was called to a Polisario office just outside the camp. He entered a dark room. Aït Chrif stood in the corner. It had been nearly a decade since he'd last talked to him.

"Word has gotten around that a particular sign was purposely left in your office," Chrif admonished.

"This is untrue, Shreef," he vociferated.

"Doctor, you know, over the years, we've never suspected any of your behavior." He spoke in the same ambiguous tone of voice he had used years prior.

Azeddine no longer feared for his life, as he once had, only of torture.

"Someone entered the infirmary before we got there," Azeddine started. "They took the typewriter, the medical reports, and two of the posters. If you had told *me* to clean up the place, I would have cleared it all out." He wasn't going to recoil in front of Chrif. "Your officers ordered me to take their blood. I do," he said in a partially defensive tone.

Chrif grabbed a metal baton off the bench and said, "I don't enjoy my position. I am so far involved in SADR. You have no idea."

What was he implying? The man was a time bomb. Was

he going to unleash his wrath upon Azeddine right then and there?

"Doctor," Chrif continued, "why haven't you tried running? Why have you helped my men?" Chrif continued tapping the baton into the palm of his hand.

"That's my job. I'm a doctor; it's what I do." Azeddine believed what he said, but also wanted to divert Chrif's attention away from the poster incident.

"You have nothing. Nothing!" Chrif glowered. "Allah left me years ago! Or, maybe it was I who left him."

Azeddine didn't know what to do. He thought about his friends who had been tortured to death in front of his own eyes over the last years. They had been loyal servants of Allah.

Pray five times a day. Kneel toward Mecca. No clean water.

Chrif slammed the baton down on the bench. His face was red with rage. He simply pointed to the door.

Azeddine stepped out into the stifling desert, hoping a breeze would come along and carry him away from this wretched place.

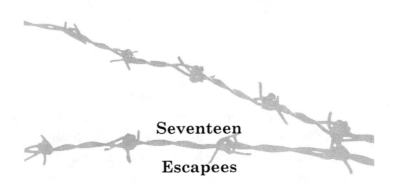

Seventeen

Escapees

The Association of Victims of Human Rights Violations in Polisario Prisons (ASVIPO) drew the attention of the international community on crimes against humanity committed by the Algeria-backed Polisario guerrilla movement.... Over 1,700 Moroccan[s]...died or disappeared as a result of the atrocities perpetrated by Polisario mercenaries, genuine enemies of people in the Moroccan Sahara, deplored the association.

- Human rights association points fingers at Polisario atrocities in Tindouf, Algeria, *Politics* 9/26/2003

AFTER MY time in the Peace Corps in 2002, before moving to Ifrane, I lived in Rabat, at the Kasbah des Oudayas, a fortress on the Atlantic Ocean. My small one-bedroom apartment was just above a Moroccan family's home. The Oudayas was unlike any other place in Rabat. It was the oldest part of this imperial city, and its mud-packed walls, winding, car-free alleys, and whitewashed homes all attested to its fortified history.

Inside the walls, I could be alone with my thoughts. From my terrace, I gazed at the stars. The sound of the ocean lulled me to sleep at night. I still didn't feel free, though. When I left the Kasbah each day to go to work as a language instructor at an English-language institute, I'd step out into the congestion of traffic and people. Cars zoomed by, not heeding pedestrians or, for that matter, other vehicles. Women clad in djellabas huddled together adorning each other with henna tattoos. Mustachioed men congregated, discussing anything from the weather to politics to the latest sporting event.

Ifrane was much quieter. On my runs through the forest, I thought about how Azeddine wasn't able to enjoy his own country. The only world he knew for so long had been the flat, barren, arid landscape filled with misery and questions. I would've tried anything to get out of there, but I know the only reason Azeddine is alive now is because he didn't run.

The International Red Cross had been trying to gain access to the prisoners for years, but before they were able to penetrate within Polisario walls, countless incidents of torture and death were inflicted upon the POWs. Ahmed revealed to Azeddine what had happened at the camps in Rabonée and Hanafi, where he had worked.

In 1981, two men were crazy enough to attempt escaping from Rabonée. Politically, it was a time when Libya signed an arms agreement with Morocco, thereby forfeiting all weapons trade with the Polisario.

The two men should have waited just a week or two longer. Lieutenant Mohamedine and Mouharir Salah were captured a couple of hours after their escape and taken to a small building outside the camp. Electrical cables soaked in water transferred 220 volts of electricity through their bodies as they were being whipped. Their screams were heard all night long. They didn't die, but they must have wished they had. Isolated from the other prisoners, they moved bricks from sunrise until past midnight, and then slept in cramped underground chambers.

"They tortured for following year," Azeddine said with an expression of disgust.

Several more prisoners tried fleeing over the next few months. If they weren't tortured to death, they ended up in Azeddine's care. Sometimes, a nurse named Zami or Nurse Omar would help him. Other times, he had to send the victims to Rabonée to be treated by Ahmed. Ahmed questioned Azeddine about their role in saving people. *Was it worth it? Did these wretched souls really want to recuperate just to be the objects of even more torment?*

Another prisoner named Amrani tried escaping the following year. The Polisario captured him while he was on the run in one of their military Land Rovers. After beating him, they tied him to the back of their truck and sped over the rocky terrain, dragging his body behind. His neck was broken, his body severely maimed, but he remained alive.

Azeddine communicated with mixed feelings that he was happy some managed to get away, but those left behind paid for the absconding few.

The camp in Hanafi, located eight miles south of Tindouf, was a military arms depot with abundant storage of all-terrain vehicles; more civilian and military POWs were being kept there. Seven of them were mechanics. They told the one guard on duty, since it was a holiday, they'd like to finish up some work on the new Toyota trucks a Spanish NGO had recently donated to the Polisario. They managed to push one of the new trucks far enough away that the guard couldn't hear the engine start. They left the remaining trucks inside the garage but broke the locks and cut the gas lines. They also opened the valves of the two gas reserves used to fuel the camps' vehicles and machinery. They weren't discovered missing until the next morning. The Polisario even notified the Algerian army. All they found were empty tracks. The Polisario Security Office brought in Amhamad Sidi Bouya, recommended by Algeria, to rectify the situation. Bouya made sure the prisoners who remained behind went without food or sleep for days. The prisoners were thinner than rails, with battered backs and blistered feet. Azeddine didn't think of Bouya as a man, but as a cold-blooded murderer responsible for the butchering of his fellow men.

A few months after their visit to Neuf Juin, in a small encampment southwest of Tindouf known as Poste Gire, ten more prisoners plotted their escape. This time, however, they managed to get the guards on their side. Azeddine wished he had been one of them. On the other hand, knowing his actions could have caused the torture and death of other prisoners would have remained on his conscience forever.

"Death not scare me. Dying is easy," Azeddine relayed midway during his telling. "How I die, though, I am scared."

Success came their way only because the Polisario Security Office had delayed their visit to the camp that week. And in that time, they convinced the guards to join their scheme. They stole a US $70,000 Mercedes Uni-mog and took off as fast as they could for the Moroccan border, to the same place the pilot had crossed. Only one guard wasn't in on it: Lemam. They left him tied up and gagged in one of the underground chambers. He couldn't move for over two days. Polisario security forces found the small post deserted; only Leman remained to recount the tale.

Four times a day, the prisoners assembled outside for roll call: at dawn, sundown, ten at night, and one in the morning. Sometimes the POW officers were exempt from the one a.m. roll call, but only if everything had run smoothly in the camp that day. On one of these nights, a clever man named Mahjoub had made his move.

As the roll call was taking place outside, Mahjoub exited the officers' quarters and didn't return. Azeddine wondered where he was going but thought nothing of it since Mahjoub often slipped away for a smoke. It had been years since any of the officers had tried anything remotely related to escape. Azeddine hoped it would stay that way.

Mahjoub was scheduled for a visit with Azeddine at noon the next day about a pulled back muscle. At three, he was supposed to see one of the visiting Cuban physicians for a more specialized consultation. The Cubans were highly educated physicians and engineers in their fields. These specialists were sent regularly to the Polisario camps as a part of Cuba's international aid initiative, set up by Fidel Castro. In doing so, Cuba and the Polisario established a trusting relationship. Some of the officers in the Polisario had even been trained in Cuba.

When there was no sign of Mahjoub during the entire morning and afternoon, Azeddine had no choice but to approach the head guard at the camp.

"Shreef, Mr. Mahjoub has not come in for his consultation. He was supposed to see me. He had another appointment this afternoon with the Cuban doctor and didn't show up."

"So, was he supposed to be under your supervision?" the guard asked.

"No, Sir. I was to meet with him at noon."

Normally, he wouldn't have notified the head guard, but if he didn't, all the prisoners inside the camp, including himself, would have suffered.

If Mahjoub had tried anything, his chances were slim to none that he'd make it out of Algeria alive, especially solo. If he did make it, the other prisoners within the camp would be interrogated and castigated by the guards until someone else was killed in his stead.

Most who did escape didn't go far. The Polisario hunted them down, killing the attempted escapee on the spot, the body left in the middle of the desert. In reports made to the NGOs, the Polisario claimed many prisoners died of natural causes. In not one report did they ever cite beating the prisoners to death or blowing their brains out with a revolver.

On occasion, there were false alarms. A suspected

eluder might be discovered sleeping under a truck or in the corner of a garage. He'd get a beating, but no one else was punished for it. Azeddine remembered what Ali had said twelve years ago, that Allah would free them; they'd all go home. No matter what Azeddine believed, prisoners planned their escape route for months—or years. The notion floated in everyone's mind.

The sun was about to set in the distance. The warmth of the day gave way to the utter chill of night. Mahjoub was nowhere to be found. Every prisoner was ordered to stand outside his quarters until Mahjoub was found. Two hours later, the prisoners still stood outside, now shivering from the onslaught of the cold desert night.

"Bring out all your possessions!" a guard thundered.

Whenever there was a search by the guards of the prisoners' possessions, they were always caught with things they shouldn't have and punished for it. Most of the time, a few cigarettes would set off the guards' fury. Only three cigarettes were allowed per person, per day. Azeddine hid his rations inside the infirmary to give to a nervous patient, or to barter for a can of sardines or powdered milk. The guards didn't say anything as long as rules were followed. But these privileges could disappear instantly if boundaries were overstepped. Prisoners brought out their blankets and thin black plastic bags of belongings and laid them on the ground. The guards circulated carrying their whips.

"Where can we find Sidi Mahjoub? If you speak now, you save everyone! Empty out your bags!"

It had taken years for the prisoners to collect the few precious things they had. Guards ripped open bags, dumping contents onto the sand.

Azeddine's real stash was in the infirmary. The bag in his hand contained nothing but a sweatshirt, a can of picante anchovies, and a few cigarettes. The prisoner beside him had a small battery-operated radio that fell out when his bag was torn open. Even if it worked, no outside signals would reach them. Immediately, the guard's whip came down on the prisoner's back, splitting his sweatshirt and slicing the skin beneath. He dropped to the ground, begging for mercy.

Once the bags were unpacked, everyone's possessions were either confiscated or trampled. Azeddine stood with his hands behind his back, counting in sets of twenty to make his fear subside and take his mind away from the bitter cold. They had found no proof of anyone knowing anything on the whereabouts of Mahjoub. It was a cold night. The guards had changed shifts and came dressed to combat the weather. The prisoners were told to report to their cells for the night.

Just before everyone gathered their blankets, a guard announced, "Lieutenant Larbi, bring your blanket and come with us." As Larbi approached, the guard continued, "We need to clarify a few things."

Azeddine didn't sleep that night, but prayed. He was scared for Larbi.

"Larbi est quelqu'un de bien…," Azeddine said to me outloud. Larbi is a good man. "I repeat ninety-nine names of Allah for him safety."

That night, Larbi was hung by the wrists from a railroad tie in an underground barracks. He was positioned with his forearms underneath his quadriceps, so that his body hung in mid-air. He was beaten with a whip, followed by a metal bar until he blacked out.

At around dawn, one blow to the head ended his life. He was buried six miles away. When the sun's rays glistened off the sand that January morning, the prisoners knew that Larbi had suffered a great deal. In the camp that morning, no one talked. Everyone mourned.

Larbi, now a martyr, was reported dead to the Red Cross. On his death report, the Polisario stated that he had tried escaping and been restrained but became too violent to control.

Azeddine thought he might start praying again in memory of Larbi. It had been a while since he had prayed at all. He needed a sign, a symbol that Allah was there with them. He closed his teary eyes in exhaustion.

Two days later, prisoners were emptying bags of millet and rice given to them by the UN into plain unmarked bags so the Polisario could sell it to Mauritania. Meant for the Moroccan POWs and Saharawi refugees, it was embezzled across the border and sold for profit. A strong odor emanated from one of the crates. Upon investigation, they found Mahjoub's body. He'd been too weak to heave the forty-pound bag of rice off his head; he suffocated as he awaited the trucks to deliver the cargo to Mauritania and him to potential freedom.

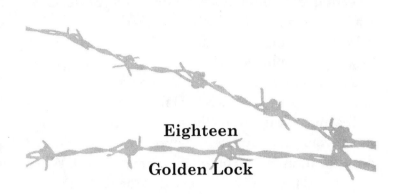

Eighteen

Golden Lock

Sir, we are writing concerning your letter from the 12th of August 1981. We have requested from the Saharawi Red Crescent any information regarding your son's detainment by the Polisario Front since August 24, 1979. On the same note, we have requested they share the letters you wrote with your son. We regret we haven't any more information about this subject....
Rest assured that we are doing everything in our ability to obtain authorization to visit all the Moroccan prisoners and that this road may allow us to gain new insights regarding your son.

- Madame R. Dufey, Chef de la Zone Afrique du Nord, Official letter from the Committee of the International Red Cross, November 24, 1981, to Azeddine's father.

AZEDDINE GAZED up from the mantel to the stairs. He saw a mirror and it made him pause. The cool breeze behind him waned, and he continued to hold the blurry images of his family in his mind. The mirror was antique. As he climbed the steps and got closer, he realized the mirror was his grandfather's.

While visiting his grandfather's house as a small boy, he remembered asking him where it came from. His grandfather told him it had come from the rolling green hills in the southwest of France.

The mirror was now on the staircase. Azeddine stood there, confused because the mirror had disappeared from the house when his grandfather had died. When he reached the mirror, he looked at the reflection. He saw a silver hallway, gray and misty, lined with mirrors. He looked down from the stairwell, but the mantel was gone. There was nothing but a dim light and more stairs going down. He didn't want to go back down, he wanted to climb up. The dream startled him. For so many years, it had been the same. He carried it with him day and night.

The Red Cross continued visiting the camps, and in 1986, Azeddine received a few letters from home. Some prisoners had packages delivered directly to them by the Red Cross. Most received clothes, especially djellabas— full-length wool robes with a cone-shaped hood. One prisoner discovered his family had cut an opening into the leather of his new sandals and placed money inside. The guards found the stash hidden in a plastic bag behind a loose brick in the wall of his hut. From then on, packages were checked before being given to the prisoners. The Red Cross objected. Coincidentally, guards showed up wearing new sweaters, djellabas, and sandals.

Azeddine wasn't sure what to do when he received his first letter. With restrained joy, he placed it in the inside pocket of his lab coat and finished up with some patients. He didn't want to read it right away, but wanted the moment to last. When the room was empty, he sat down and unfolded it. The letter was in his father's handwriting but signed at the bottom by his whole family. It was simple, revealing a mixture of sadness and hope:

> We miss you to no end. Each of us pray five times a day for your protection. It's the only thing I ask of Allah now. We received word that you are stationed in a camp where you can help your fellow Moroccans. I know that you are doing your best. Remember that dream I told you about before you went to Casablanca? I still have it, but it's different now. I wish I could have explained it to you before you left. In my dreams, I know you will be free. I hold your picture close to my heart before I go to sleep. When I wake up, I place it next to the Koran in a box I carved while sitting alone at our favorite café. We miss you, my son. We love you.

Azeddine folded the letter, put it back in his pocket, and sat in shock, overwhelmed by the effect of it all. He would write his family the next day, he decided. He didn't want to do it now; it would be too emotional for him. He didn't want to pour out his feelings to them or mention all the suffering he and his comrades had been through over all those years. It would cause them too much grief. He didn't know what to say. He wanted to outline it in his head before he wrote it, stressing the fact that he was fine and they need not worry.

He went to bed thinking about what his father had said in the letter. Before Azeddine left for Casablanca, he remembered that, early one morning, while it was still dark outside, his father came into his room. He whispered to him that he was worried about his going to the Sahara, that he had had a nightmare.

His father had never really talked about his dreams before then. In his father's visions, he was reaching out for Azeddine, but couldn't grab him because the dimensions between them kept on changing. He reached for his son, but disappeared from his grasp.

On his cot, Azeddine opened the letter and placed it over his heart, just like his father had done with his photo. He wasn't sure what it all meant. He closed his eyes and shed tears of relief, joy, sadness, confusion, and anguish. They were emotions that had been bottled up inside of him for all those years.

Throughout the summer of 1987, life in the camp continued as normal. The prisoners had heard rumors of the sand wall being built across the desert frontier, which would make it difficult for the Polisario to continue their ground attacks on the small villages along the border. The United Nations were in the process of forming a special investigative committee to look at possible resolutions to this conflict.

Azeddine wrote three letters home over the next few months but received none in response. Maybe they hadn't gotten his letters. In April, a letter came for him postmarked from France. On it was his cousin's name, followed by the initials "M. D." His younger cousin had become a doctor and was now working in France. He couldn't wait to read the letter in the infirmary; he unfolded it where he was and read:

My Dear Azeddine,

I'm sorry to have to be the one to tell you this, especially in the form of a letter, but there is no other way. Your mother and sister contacted me and asked me to write. For some reason, they believed that I would know how to word the following message.

Your father, my uncle, passed away during the night. He was being treated at the best private clinic in Fez. The doctor worked hard to save him, but could not. Your family will pay no medical expenses for his stay. The doctor paid all costs out of his own pocket. Your mother, sister, and brother are in mourning. They couldn't tell you he had been sick for some time; that is why they didn't write. We love you and pray for you daily.

Yours, Mohammed.

As he dropped the letter, he dropped to his knees. The guards and prisoners stopped to look as he righted himself, grabbed the letter, and ran to the infirmary.

"Allah! Allah!" was what the guards heard emanating from Azeddine's quarters.

A guard entered and quickly left. Azeddine rocked back and forth on a chair, gripping his head and sobbing uncontrollably until he toppled to the ground. He got up, picked up the small butane stove, and hurled it on top of the fallen chair.

"ALLAH," he wheezed between sobs. He got on his knees, holding his father's letter between his hands. He felt like tearing it to pieces, but couldn't. His hands looked like his father's; they trembled the same way his father's had. The letter slipped out of his grip as he continued staring at his hands. Another guard entered the room and seized him by the elbows. Azeddine didn't resist. He just held his head down, tears falling onto the dirt floor.

"J'étais impuissant—" Azeddine mumbled as tears streamed down his face. "I want to be near my mother to comfort her."

He lay on his cot inside the infirmary in a stupor. He was physically and mentally numb.

Throughout the evening and into the night, numerous prisoners stopped to offer their condolences. A guard he had treated two weeks earlier dropped by and gave him a bag of louiza, a type of verbena tea. He thought back to the guard's jeep accident.

"The guard tell me," Azeddine said, getting misty eyed, "he told me he wanted me to have freedom to go home. My father maybe alive if I there. He has 56 years and died. He had a broken heart."

His comrades recited the Koran outside his door during the night. He shut his eyes and breathed slowly.

"Je ne peux pas … ." He would never forget his father or forgive his captors.

Part Four: Sovereignty

Let us bring up the case of Dr. Azeddine Benmansour, a general practitioner who was captured in 1979, who was simply completing his military service in the Moroccan military.... After speaking to Dr. Benmansour, imprisoned in the Douze Octobre, he has already shown signs of losing the better part of his hearing [due to] abuse and torture by the Polisario.

- "Hommage au Dr. Benmansour." *Aujourd'hui.* [Newspaper in Morocco]. November 11, 2003.

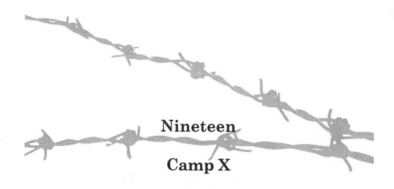

Nineteen

Camp X

AFTER RECOUNTING his father's death, Azeddine wanted to take a break from our interviews. We had been meeting for several months, and I could feel he was reliving each moment of the story as he told it to me. I also felt overwhelmed. The more Azeddine told, the more it disturbed me. During these months, I missed my brother. He had just finished his Master's Degree and decided that his credentials were good enough to get a job as a bartender in the Virgin Islands. During one of our phone conversations, he suggested I come for a visit. It didn't take much coaxing. I needed some time off too.

Three weeks on the island-paradise of St. John left me rejuvenated. "Don't I have the best office in the world," my brother said as he grilled hamburgers and served drinks. From his open-air shack perched atop a hill, tourists came to admire the bird's-eye view of the neighboring isles surrounded in crystalline waters. We played Frisbee in an open yard near the smallish port that was lined with both old and new boats.

A sea captain with a dilapidated vessel stamped our passports and took us into the British Isles for twenty dollars. The British-owned isles were more remote and much prettier, or better maintained, than their American counterparts. One of the islands belonged to a family, a gift from the Queen. We landed on Cooper Island where we lunched on conch-shell biscuits and snorkeled near what many claim was Robert Louis Stevenson's Treasure Island. My brother refuted the claim, and I wasn't about to contest. He had read over 30 adventure-travel novels in the last three months, especially those relating to the sea. Before my departure back to Morocco, he decided he would come and join me and stay throughout the summer in North Africa.

After our break, Azeddine was ready to get back to our interviews. He said he had been learning to drive and was thinking of getting his own apartment. I gave him some furniture I didn't need, and we moved it into his mother's spare bedroom. During our first session back, he said he had fasted the whole month we had been apart and he felt better than ever.

"Juste huit ans à rattraper!" he joked; only eight more years of fasting to catch up on. He admitted he hadn't always been able to observe the month-long fast of Ramadan while in the Sahara.

The more he revealed, the more I learned how patient and persevering he was.

The Polisario's dirty secret was now exposed thanks to Azeddine's poster ploy. They still attacked the border but did so with less ferocity than earlier. The Red Cross was paying more visits to the camps.

Human Rights Watch remained one of the only organizations that continued voicing their support for the Polisario. In what became their most extensive mission to the camps, the organization found that since some of the most ruthless leaders had been ousted from the camps, conditions were improving and were "satisfactory," save for the continued mistreatment of the Moroccan POWs.

The Polisario concentrated more than ever on improving their image now that they were in the limelight of the international community. Algeria supported the Polisario; Western Sahara was their gateway to gaining access to the Atlantic Ocean. But Algeria had problems of its own. They were getting tired of heavily funding an organization that couldn't survive on its own, especially when their own country was on the brink of civil war.

Azeddine was working double time, being trucked between the Neuf Juin and Douze Octobre camps. In Neuf Juin, he treated a Saharawi man who was also a prisoner. He couldn't figure out why the Polisario had treated one of their own so horribly.

"His name was Sarokhe, or Rocket," Azeddine said with a smile.

After giving the man a routine check-up, Azeddine wasn't sure what this man had undergone, but from his condition, it was substantial.

"He need the food et vitamines," Azeddine said.

Sarokhe was aptly named. He stood well over six-

and-a-half feet, quite tall for someone who looked to be of Berber descent. Known as "Rocketman," he mentioned that he was actually a native Saharawi, from a small town on the Moroccan side of the Moroccan-Algerian border, a tribune called Izarguryane.

Azeddine asked him in Darija, "If you're a Saharawi, why didn't you come across into Algeria with all the other refugees?"

"I refused. I took my family the opposite direction. I wanted to go to the Atlas Mountains. I wanted no part of this life here: being a refugee, living in camps, and told what to do."

"What happened?" Rocketman proceeded to undress so Azeddine could take a closer look at him. Before him stood the emaciated frame of a man, reminiscent of photos he'd seen back in medical school of those suffering extreme malnutrition and starvation.

"They captured me while they were patrolling my village. I wasn't doing anything out of the ordinary. They brought me to Rabonée, questioned me, and told me I had no choice. I would have to marry here," Rocketman continued in his dialect from the eastern part of Morocco, slightly different but comprehensible. "I told them I wasn't going to stay. They said, 'You are Saharawi; it's your duty,' then took me to Camp Errachid."

Azeddine listened in shock. He had heard about this camp, but hadn't been sure if it existed or not. Camp Errachid was named after a Polisario leader who had died in battle. The camp was also known as Camp Inconnu, the Unknown Camp, or Camp X. He wanted to find out everything he could about what Rocketman had experienced there without seeming too intrusive.

"They kept you there?"

"They kept me there for a long time. There were other Moroccans there too."

"They have Moroccans there? Where is the camp?" Azeddine asked as he cleaned a needle.

"It's ten miles from Smara, twenty miles from Douze Octobre. I wished for death every day. I slept in a five-by-five-foot steel container. We were forced to make bricks, barefoot. Some men roasted out there. The bodies, we threw them in a hole and covered them up with dirt as if nothing had happened."

"Why did they let you go?"

"I was ready to be one of them, and here I am." He held out his frail arms.

This was the first Saharawi Azeddine had seen who had been treated as bad as or worse than the Moroccan prisoners. Rocketman's first job, he admitted, once rehabilitated, was to round up Moroccan prisoners to talk and sing over the loudspeakers. This would be his first test of allegiance to the Polisario.

Azeddine hoped he wouldn't have to speak over the system, like Aït Chrif had mentioned years ago. It would be easier for him to do his job if he could feign neutrality. He went out and handed the guard a copy of Rocketman's prescription. He also slipped him three cigarettes. The guard put them in his front pocket and walked inside the infirmary to take Rocketman to the compound where he would receive some of the nourishment he needed.

The slander over the loudspeakers began a week later. Sarokhe's job was to take Moroccan prisoners to publicly profess their hatred for Morocco and its king, followed by admittance that the Polisario were the rightful inhabitants of Western Sahara. If a prisoner refused, punishment was severe.

Sarokhe entered the infirmary for the second time, telling Azeddine he would have to declare his allegiance the next day. He didn't look Azeddine in the eyes. Azeddine argued he had too much work for this type of nonsense. He told Sarokhe if the Polisario wanted him to speak over their radio, they'd have to ship him away first, leaving them with no doctor in both camps to take care of their medical needs or emergencies.

Azeddine was lucky; by chance or by design, he never was called again.

Some months later, Rocketman had amassed enough money in some fashion to convince a guard to drive him to the sand wall. Rocketman made it back into Morocco and returned to his family. Azeddine imagined himself, like Sarokhe, crossing the border and going home.

In 1991, the United Nations called a cease-fire to the Sahara conflict. MINURSO, the organization that would oversee it all, was established. It became the United Nation's Mission for Referendum in Western Sahara, to control the situation between Morocco and the Polisario.

James Baker from the US was appointed head of this venture. His role was to make sure both sides adhered to the UN's newly imposed regulations. The questions most observers had were: Would this part of the world finally be its own independent nation, or would it be considered "Greater Morocco"? Were they really going to resolve the situation? And when? Or did they just want to tap into the phosphate mines and oil reserves?

By this time, the Red Cross had registered over half the prisoners in the camps, with the exception of Camp X. They didn't know about its existence until more prisoners started speaking up, disclosing its possible location. Azeddine was taken there just after the ceasefire. He had wondered why no one had ever been able to pinpoint its exact location, but once he arrived, he understood. He stood between two large sand dunes. Sand blew at his feet. The ground showed no sign of vegetation or civilization.

Bulldozers and forklifts hauled sand over metal boxcars. In another section was a medium-sized bunker. After getting nearer, he saw eyes looking at him from inside. Fifteen prisoners were being kept there, including Mustapha. He looked gaunt and weather-beaten, the skin on his face was withered and taut, and his lips were unusually swollen. Azeddine diagnosed his symptoms immediately. He needed to be hooked up to an intravenous line of saline solution to hydrate his body.

The Polisario officials told Azeddine to examine the prisoners individually so he could write detailed reports of their health conditions. Afterward, they were to be shipped to Rabonée for treatment and then dispersed throughout the other camps. With more international attention, the Polisario had to cover up their misdeeds.

Just as he was examining Mustapha, Azeddine felt a blow to the right side of his head. He felt unsteady, as if he were going to fall. The room began to spin. His ear throbbed in intense pain. He heard ringing inside his head. He turned and looked up to see a guard standing above him. The guard's lips moved, but he couldn't hear. Blood dripped from his ear onto his shoulder. He knelt on the ground and cupped his hand over his ear. The guard jabbed him with his baton. He didn't move, still in shock from the blow.

He knew something had gone wrong. He couldn't hear anything. The guard who had brought Azeddine ran over and shoved the offending guard against the wall. He took the doctor to another small bunker with a bed where he rested, though his head pounded and his ear still rang. All he wanted was water, a blanket, and to be left alone.

Two days later, the bulldozers continued to rumble. Azeddine's right ear was extremely sensitive and had turned purple, but he could hear a little better out of it despite the persistent tinnitus. He continued to listen to the accounts of torture that had taken place in Camp X; numerous swore the same stories, such as the insertion of insects into their ears and sand slowly sprinkled in their eyes. They also mentioned they were used in various strange experiments.

By 1993, the Red Cross had finally seen most of the prisoners from Camp X; many had been scattered throughout the camps. A few NGOs sent out teams to investigate Camp X's remains. While some remnants of boxcars were found, no bodies were ever recovered.

Azeddine vowed that one day he would dedicate a monument to their memory. His damaged ear and decreased hearing were permanent reminders—souvenirs—of the time he'd spent there. Now he knew; the torture that went on at Camp X was real. It was not a made-up story simply created to scare prisoners.

The men who died there had once stood proud beside their families, had vied for the betterment of their homeland, and were thereafter forced to brave the worst perils as POWs. They were then to perish far from their homes, forgotten by the rest of the world.

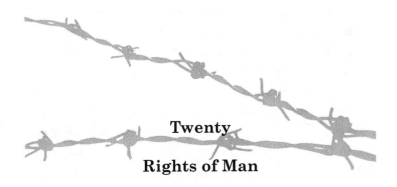

Twenty

Rights of Man

Late 1980s to mid 1990s

AZEDDINE RETURNED to Douze Octobre after his time at Camp X. Each man detained there, POW or Saharawi, bore the scars to testify to Camp X's existence. The Polisario, for now, had successfully covered up their iniquities.

His nightmares became infused with images of Batal, Camp X, injured comrades, and ghostly beings rising from their bloody sheets. *How could any human being create such a vile reality?* Hardly any prisoners held resentment toward Morocco. But some would question the kingdom's ability to fathom the harsh cruelty prisoners underwent. *Would the families and friends of those who died within the camps ever learn the bitter truth behind their deaths?*

While financial aid from world organizations continued pouring in to help the Polisario cause, various construction projects were in progress. The building and rebuilding of new and old camps was at the top of the agenda. Azeddine was so busy, he instantly fell asleep the minute he lay on his cot, but the stress and fatigue still overtook him during the day.

He began having serious lower-back pain. Weeks prior, he had passed a kidney stone, but this pain was more overpowering, more debilitating. One night when the pain was so sharp, he became dizzy, rolled off his cot, and knocked himself cold when he hit the floor. The next morning, the diabetic prisoner who had come for his insulin shot found Azeddine face down in the dirt.

Rushed to the military hospital in Rabonée, Ahmed was by his side when he awoke. Ahmed told him something that he didn't understand. Nurses rushed him by gurney to the emergency ward.

"Is it another kidney stone?" Azeddine asked on the way.

"C'est l'edema!" Ahmed panted down at him.

In the emergency center, Ahmed scribbled his signature on the necessary forms. The hospital was reserved for the care of the Polisario. Only in an extreme emergency was a Moroccan POW granted treatment. Azeddine was valuable to them. If they didn't keep their doctors healthy, they'd have no one to patch the prisoners well enough to keep them working.

"You can do the tests," Azeddine told Ahmed in French. "My legs and feet are swollen. I can feel the fluid in my knees." His elbows ached too, but, he thought, it might be a false alarm.

"Moi, I not meant to be patient," Azeddine admitted

as he and I walked the streets of Fez, the first time we had talked freely while walking outside together. He had always felt it was his job to help patients, not be one.

"Five sick patients are in need of my care back in Douze Octobre."

"The swelling may be contained in your legs now, but we have to make sure it's not going to spread." Ahmed paused, then added, "Your patients will be looked after. It's you we need to keep an eye on for now."

Azeddine was happy to see Ahmed, even under the circumstances. He wished he could've spent more quality time with him. If they ever made it back home, no one could stop them from meeting at a café and talking. They'd meet everyday if they wanted.

"I don't want this to reach your lungs. Let's start with some diuretics."

Despite Azeddine's knowledge of the procedure, he appreciated Ahmed's words.

"You know, my dad," Azeddine continued with a grunt as he re-positioned himself on the gurney, "died of a broken heart, heart failure." Azeddine didn't know why he'd mentioned that. Perhaps he felt death was near.

"You could've lost a part of your heart when your father died. But, there's enough heart inside you to fight this off." Ahmed pressed the stethoscope to Azeddine's chest.

"I wish the Red Cross could've helped us communicate. My sister said my father wrote them letters every single week. The Red Cross always responded with the same news—no news."

"When you're better and back on your toes, pay the Red Cross a visit."

Azeddine leaned his head back to think for a moment.

"You're going to need to rest for a while. Your liver and kidneys will recover, but you'll need plenty of water and protein," Ahmed prescribed. "I'll find a way to get all the care you'll need for a quick recovery."

"Could you also bring me a small bell so I can ring for you," Azeddine teased.

"Your tongue is what should have swelled up!" Ahmed retorted.

Ahmed was right; bed rest was necessary for an extended amount of time. His edema was serious but treatable. Due to the conditions in the camps, Azeddine had to recover fully in the hospital. Outside, any bug, ailment, or virus could manifest itself, taking a serious toll on his health if he was still weakened by edema.

"We'll check your urine during the next seventy-two hours. Hopefully, drinking lots of water and getting your protein levels back up will take care of it." Ahmed looked at Azeddine. "Have you donated blood recently?"

"The guards come at two in the morning and demand that I wake the men to extract their blood, even during Ramadan. That's not a donation."

"It's not," Ahmed sighed. "Has blood been extracted illegally from your body lately? It might explain why there's blood in your urine."

"No, not for a long time."

It took forty-two days, but Azeddine recovered and

returned to his camp. During his time in the hospital, under Ahmed's care, he had a renewed sense of hope that he would see his family again. Ahmed was the only person he truly trusted. If anything should happen to Ahmed, Azeddine thought he would plunge into an abyss of despair. Beyond that, a stalwart faith in Allah was the only thing he and the other prisoners had to get them through rough times.

Four years passed. The Polisario still attacked the Moroccan border and brought back prisoners, but the ceasefire had slowed their raids. Moreover, Algeria was no longer sending them as much aid or weaponry. Algeria knew since these people could survive the outermost regions of the desert, they could easily survive any such shortage of food or supplies. What they didn't think of, however, was that this lack affected the prisoners even more profoundly, for they were literally at the bottom of the pecking order. The only hope was increased external aid. The Polisario had to rekindle the outside world's flame for their cause.

It couldn't have been better timing to allow some of the prisoners to go home. NGOs would undoubtedly contribute money for the cause. Plus, a percentage of the prisoners were older, meaning that their debilitations could hinder the Polisario's mantra of always pushing forward.

High-ranking Polisario officers decided to hold a press conference announcing the release of POWs back to Morocco. The Polisario knew that King Hassan II would reject any such release; a partial release of the prisoners was unacceptable, it was all or nothing. It was an opportune time for the Polisario to act. Their calculations proved accurate.

The directors of each camp were told to choose the oldest and weakest among the prisoners, but no officers. Two hundred in total were chosen and transported to Douze Octobre. The POWs themselves weren't sure what was happening, but they were well fed and clothed.

One of these prisoners, who hadn't been allowed access to the Red Cross, was Tabia. When he was captured in 1977, his health evaluation was normal. But, after years of malnourishment and torture, he began to show signs, as Azeddine documented, of "schizophrenia and extreme hallucinations." Some nights Azeddine found him asleep on the ground outside the infirmary. The other prisoners took care of him like a brother, sharing their food, shelter, and clothing with him; they helped him go to the bathroom and take a shower, among other things. The guards allowed him to wander around the camp. He never hurt anyone or anything.

A guard named Mrabih or "Haj" (as it was thought that he had visited Mecca) entered Tabia's tent one night and cajoled him outside. Haj drove him out into the desert, shot him, and buried his body in the sand. The next morning the guards were on full alert: Tabia had *escaped*!

"I not sure if all guards know, but many know he dead," Azeddine recalled.

They found no trace of Tabia. He hadn't been capable of escaping. If he had wandered outside the camp, Azeddine believed, he would have sat by the gate until they let him back in.

Some months later, a violent Sirocco storm swept through the area, uncovering Tabia's body. The next day, a truckload of prisoners passing by noticed the body and asked the driver to stop.

Azeddine later learned that Algeria had actually mandated Tabia's death; they couldn't return a prisoner who had lost his mind as a result of being in their camps.

Mohamed Khadade, the new head of Polisario security, saw to it that all activity between prisoners be closely monitored in order to prevent any unforeseen problems for the Polisario and their mission.

After the Polisario announced the release of the 200 prisoners, the Moroccan king demanded that all the prisoners be released. The Polisario got exactly what they'd wanted. When King Hassan II didn't allow their repatriation, the Polisario built another camp about ten miles outside of Rabonée called Brahim Serfati. NGOs gave them money, food, rice, and chickens so these feeble old men could take care of themselves. The Polisario now considered them *free* and out of their hands. The Polisario hoarded a high percentage of the supplies nonetheless, but at least the men got something.

For the first few months, the prisoners were doing well at Brahim Serfati. They built themselves shacks and planted a vegetable garden. However, after so many years of being tortured, underfed, and enslaved, these men neither had the strength nor the energy to withstand the remaining years of their lives in the desert without medical attention.

Over the next years, after the United States had sent delegates, the king finally succumbed. One of those representatives was Madeline Albright, the US Ambassador to the UN and soon to become the US Secretary of State. The French government, along with several NGOs, worked on the prisoners' behalf as well. Argentina even became heavily involved in the negotiations.

Several elderly prisoners had already died when they were finally allowed back into Morocco. Only 185 remained of the original 200 sequestered at Brahim Serfati to see their families again. Azeddine was heartbroken that the fifteen who died never made it home. He believed King Hassan II was diligently working for them to be freed, in spite of demanding all the prisoners held in Algeria be released at the same time. But the Polisario still had a few more years of blood and labor to extract from the almost 2000 POWs that remained.

After the first 185 prisoners were accepted back into Morocco, the next batch to be released didn't anticipate any problems. The Polisario thought they had cleared the path for future releases of those they no longer needed. Polisario intelligence chose ninety more aged or ailing prisoners to be sent to Brahim Serfati, for an eventual release back to Morocco. Again, the king didn't allow any of them entrance back into the country. For two years, the prisoners waited in Brahim Serfati as their predecessors had.

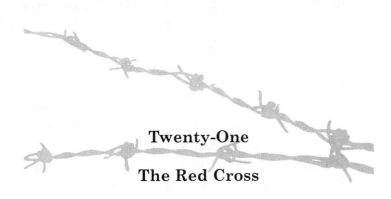

Twenty-One

The Red Cross

MY TWIN decided to come spend the last two months with me in Ifrane before my summer vacation at the school. My interviews with Azeddine continued, and he wanted to meet my brother. He invited both of us over for lunch, and I did my best at being the unofficial translator. Terry was surprised at how well Azeddine was adjusting; Morocco had definitely changed in 24 years.

Terry was so intrigued and riveted by the whole ordeal that I asked him if he wanted to go on a field trip to Western Sahara. We didn't have time for the two-day bus ride south, so we opted for the US $250 roundtrip plane ticket instead. We would soon be in Laayoune, capital of Western Sahara. I wanted to see for myself what MINURSO, regulated by the UN, was doing for the prisoners. For ten years the organization had been there, the contention of the Sahara still unresolved.

The pilot-in-training landed us safely enough despite

the rocky touchdown. We took a taxi sgher, a small taxi, to a hotel that cost four dollars a night. At two in the morning, when we heard soldiers trudging up and down the stairs, girls in tow, we knew we'd get no more sleep.

We searched for another hotel the next morning. After finding one that cost nearly US $30, we headed for MINURSO's office. Rows of white trucks with the UN emblem on the doors lined the exterior of the building, which was surrounded by a razor-wire fence. Guards stood outside and asked what we wanted. I told them we wanted to talk to someone in charge and I showed them a piece of paper with names I had jotted down on it. They were all, of course, on vacation, and if I wanted to see someone in charge, I would have to go to their branch in Casablanca. Plan B: I decided to see the governor, the Caid of Laayoune. He should be able to answer some questions and, hopefully, he wasn't on vacation.

In Morocco, it's best to show up to places unannounced. The "Inshallah Principle," as we came to call it, was in full effect, especially at the government level. Things happened, Inshallah, God-willing. At the governor's office, we were well received and taken to an office where we got to speak with Rashid, the Moroccan head of MINURSO. I let on that I was a graduate student in Middle Eastern affairs interested in knowing why the prisoners were still being held in Algeria and why MINURSO wasn't getting them out.

Rashid rambled on, in French, about the history of the conflicts in the Sahara. I had already researched most of it on my own; my brother seemed bored out of his mind. We wanted answers, not historical mumbo jumbo.

After Rashid's chronological depiction of events, which took no less than two hours, I thanked him, feeling like I'd gotten nowhere. Second in command, his assistant, also named Rashid, told us he'd like to meet up for dinner. We didn't refuse. Rashid drove a small white car with a bad muffler and stopped by his family's grocery store to pick up a few things for dinner. At the UN apartments, we discussed the *real* situation in Western Sahara.

He told us he was sort of a diplomat who aided the communication between MINURSO and the Moroccan government. He reaffirmed that politics had gotten in the way of the bigger picture. Questions were left unanswered. How would the organization deal with the Polisario? And, what about the refugees who claimed Saharawi lineage, but also claimed to be Moroccan? The Saharawi people have a distinct culture of their own: their language, food, dress, and customs are unlike those in Fez, Marrakesh, or Rabat.

Rashid mentioned that most of the political concern over Western Sahara was attributed to the phosphate mines and the thousands of miles of Atlantic coastline. He was well suited as a quasi diplomat, who came across as truly caring about the problems of this region. It was his job, he told us later, to help the Red Cross take Moroccan Saharawis into Algeria to visit their families who were now refugees.

Rashid drove us back to our hotel and told us he had taken care of the bill for the next few days. Surprised, we couldn't thank him enough. He appreciated our concern for Western Sahara. I now saw the Saharawi refugees in a different light. This stalemate had persisted for so long. It wasn't their fault. They weren't the ones responsible for stalling referendums or decreasing monetary aid. Figuratively speaking, MINURSO was preaching peace at the podium but stalling when real issues were presented. I held firm that the Moroccan prisoners should be released and those missing accounted for. If the refugees wanted to return to Morocco, they should be able to do so or vice-versa.

Moroccan soldiers were stationed in Laayoune, but American vehicles were everywhere. I had a preconceived notion Laayoune would be more run down and not as developed as the cities up north in Morocco. But the city was modern, with hotels, restaurants, Internet cafés, and palm-tree-lined avenues. On the other hand, on the outskirts of the city, we saw the corrugated-metal and cinder block dwellings of the Moroccans who had set up camp since the Green March in 1975. We also saw the dome-shaped structures, like Azeddine had described, which made living in the desert's manic environment feasible. We took a cab ride around the city for 25 dirhams. The sand dunes were inching their way across the newly paved roads. One day, a road was covered. The next, a plow had cleared the path.

We flew back to Ifrane to the cool mountain air. I still had a lot to learn from Azeddine, but at least now, I had a better understanding of the politics behind his story and could say I had been to its setting.

Mid to late 1990s

By the end of 1994, the International Red Cross had seen nearly all the prisoners; those the Polisario had wanted them to see. Azeddine had met with them briefly in 1989, and again in 1994. Their meetings had been short and overseen by a Polisario guard.

He had waited patiently to see them, and they were finally coming to his camp again; it was 1998. Hopefully, they would bring good news from his homeland. He couldn't wait to hear about Morocco, his family, and the World Cup. He was excited just to talk to anyone from the outside. He also hoped, somehow, that he'd get the opportunity to tell them more about the daily conditions of the prisoners. The Red Cross had already found out about the illegal blood extractions. Azeddine wanted to reveal even more.

The Polisario had entrusted him to be the Red Cross' guide during their stay. When he saw the white Land Rover pull into the camp, he prepared himself. Dr. Damien, whom he had met before, climbed out of the truck. The other members brought healthy new faces.

"Azeddine, mon cher ami," Dr. Damien said.

Azeddine shook hands with him, exchanged bisous, and patted his hand over his heart.

"He from German," Azeddine let me know.

"This," Dr. Damien continued in French, holding an open hand toward the two other doctors standing beside him, "is Dr. Maurice and Dr. Giles, an ophthalmologist and a dentist, the best specialists around. "And this," he said, now pointing at Azeddine while looking at the other two, "is Dr. Azeddine Benmansour. He's helped us a great deal during our past visits."

Azeddine didn't think he had helped them all that much. Last time, when Dr. Damien was at the camp, Azeddine had arranged a work area for him, which was all.

"C'est un vrai honneur," Azeddine reenacted the scene for me; he stretched out his hand and mimicked shaking the other two doctors' hands. It was truly an honor he'd told them.

Dr. Maurice had a square jaw and graying hair combed over to the side. He was a robust man who proudly stood his ground, even though he wasn't the least bit pompous. He was wearing a blue, striped shirt tucked neatly into his jeans. His sleeves were rolled up. Dr. Giles was the exact opposite. He was short and slight with an unkempt gray beard. He wore rectangular glasses and had a pointed chin. He looked older than Dr. Maurice, but he had a more youthful air combined with a private quietude about him.

"I'll take you to your quarters for the night," Azeddine offered. A Polisario guard stood watching, but wasn't close enough to hear what they were saying. This particular guard spoke French. The Polisario made sure they chose someone who spoke French to monitor the doctors and Azeddine.

The next day, the doctors carried boxes out of their truck into the infirmary. The makeshift ward had been constructed two months earlier; the outside needed painting, the roof wasn't yet complete, and the entrance still needed a door. Azeddine couldn't believe all the fancy equipment they carried into the once empty room.

"It's all yours when we leave," Dr. Giles said as they

carried in more boxes. "Take good care of it until we come back next time."

The machinery had the Red Crescent symbol on it. Boxes were filled with surgical gloves, napkins, metal chains with clips, bandages, gauze, and other small tools. Azeddine wanted to hide it so the Polisario wouldn't come and take most of it the minute the doctors left.

That night, he and a few other prisoners were allowed to eat with the three doctors. They sat on the floor and ate out of a common platter under one fluorescent bulb. It was a meat tajine, potatoes and onions doused with paprika, salt, and cumin.

"I no eat like that for long time." It reminded Azeddine of the meal that had lain before Batal years prior.

During dinner, Dr. Damien discussed how they would have to secure the roof so flies wouldn't come in during an operation and contaminate the area. Azeddine was enjoying the freshest bread he'd had in twenty years but took time to tell Dr. Damien that he and some men would fix the roof first thing the next morning. By the end of the evening, the doctors sat drinking mint tea and determined what equipment they'd be able to start using immediately. Once the roof was secure, they'd be able to start doing the dental and eye work they had planned to get done during this visit.

Dr. Damien and Dr. Maurice headed for Rabonée to work with Ahmed for a few days while the roof was being sealed. After that, Dr. Damien stayed in Rabonée, and Dr. Maurice returned to Azeddine's camp, loaded with two boxes full of glasses to give the prisoners after their eye examinations and possible operations.

Dr. Maurice examined several of the prisoners' eyes while Azeddine assisted. After two hours, Azeddine heard the other doctor ranting to himself.

"I cannot believe the damage here!" Dr. Maurice said as he slammed his fist on the desk. "These men have been plagued! They've had no vitamin A, their eyes are filled with cataracts, and most of them are suffering from glaucoma." He called Azeddine over, "Do these men work outside during sand storms?"

"Well," Azeddine said, and then looked over his shoulder to see if the guard was nearby. "We've never been excused from labor on account of weather."

"My God!" Dr. Maurice sighed.

"I was not eye doctor," Azeddine admitted. He could not have fully assessed the damage as well as Dr. Maurice or Giles. "I know beaucoup, but I not study eyes or teeth."

"This is going to slow us down," Dr. Maurice said. He sat down on the metal chair and wiped the sweat off of his forehead. "I'm going to have to put in a request to stay longer. If not, I'll have to make another visit soon. We didn't bring enough prescription eyeglasses or sunglasses."

A few days later, Azeddine had bad news for Dr. Maurice: neither he nor Dr. Giles would be allowed to return for at least six months, and there was no guarantee they'd be allowed to return then, either. Both doctors were disillusioned, baffled that the Polisario weren't going to let them help these men.

"It costs them nothing for Christ's sake!" Dr. Maurice fumed.

That night in his hut, he told Azeddine he'd resolved to do what he could.

"Tell me, Azeddine. What the hell is going on here?" Dr. Maurice beseeched.

Azeddine checked outside the makeshift door, a piece of tin that kept sand from blowing in. "I wouldn't be able to tell you everything that has been going on here, over all these years, if I were given a year to relate it to you."

"Talk to me if you feel comfortable."

"There have been the illegal blood extractions, you know about that. These prisoners you are looking at here aren't all from this camp. They are being transported from other camps—those camps the Red Cross doesn't know exist." The scene of the bulldozers burying Camp X shot through his mind.

"Where are these camps?"

"All over. Some are small posts with only a few men, like at camp Tifaretti and Birlahlou."

Azeddine told him what he could in the limited amount of time he had. He also let Dr. Maurice know the Polisario opened letters and checked packages belonging to the prisoners, sometimes keeping the contents as a "donation."

Dr. Maurice shook his head in disbelief. Azeddine felt that the information he was telling Dr. Maurice really affected him. It seemed that these doctors were concerned about the prisoners.

Azeddine went to the flimsy tin door and hung up a green curtain to keep out flies and other unwanted pests.

"Are these death certificates accurate? I see many

were either an accident or a result of cancer."

"Only one or two died of cancer. The accidents, all cover-ups."

"All those documents we have been recording from Rabonée are useless!" Dr. Maurice sat silently.

"I want to say the truth to Dr. Maurice," Azeddine said under his breath while looking up at me from his slouched position on the couch.

Throughout their initial visit, Dr. Giles and Dr. Maurice treated as many prisoners as they could, including the Saharawi refugees. Many of the prisoners suffered some sort of ailment that was hygiene related. Numerous suffered eye infections, rotting teeth, reactions to lice, and hepatitis. The Polisario, after seeing how dedicated and focused these doctors were (even at 16 hours per day), granted them permission to return in six months. Following their second visit, however, Dr. Maurice was banned from returning to the camps. The Polisario believed he was a spy with the French government.

During the scorching summer of 1999, the prisoners learned of the death of King Hassan II. His eldest son, Crown-Prince Mohammed VI, would be the new king. To prevent riots, the Polisario ordered each prisoner to remain inside his tent, shelter, or hut. Over the next several nights, the desert air was filled with the sounds of the Koran. Someone lightly strummed a lute under one of the clearest nights Azeddine could recall. Mourning the passing of their king, the prisoners felt death even closer and longed even more for their homeland.

Twenty-Two

Against Themselves

Experts presented ... at a conference at the University of Geneva regarding the menace of the Polisario and the crisis of their transformation [toward terrorism] and what it will mean for the country [of Morocco], along with the fundamentals of democracy, not only for the Maghreb region of Africa, but equally for the rest of the world.

- *L'Opinion*, Saturday, April 3, 2004. Newspaper distributed in Morocco, France, Belgium, Tunisia, and Algeria.

IN THE summer of 2004, my brother and I went backpacking through Western Europe. A month before leaving Morocco, I wrote letters to the two Red Cross doctors that had been to Azeddine's camp, Dr. Maurice and Dr. Giles. I wrote that we would eventually be in France; we wanted to visit. They wrote back and were willing to talk. We headed up the Southern coast of

Spain into France, setting up our tents in random fields along the way.

From a small town with cobblestone roads and a truly medieval feel, I called Dr. Maurice to let him know I was in France. We arranged to meet in Paris the following week.

While my travel mates waited at a nearby park, I met Dr. Maurice for lunch at "la Coupole," a chic Parisian restaurant in the 14th arrondissement. We'd be able to have a private conversation. He talked about his time with the Red Cross and his deep concern for the Moroccans being held prisoner in the desert.

"The Polisario are unbelievably stupid. They turned away free aid," he said, scanning the room as if he were waiting for someone. "And, the Spanish, they are contributing to their terrorism."

He reached over and grabbed a light blue gift bag that was on the chair beside him; inside were newspapers and other documents.

"Take these. Use them. You didn't get them from anyone. Return them to the address provided inside when you're done," Dr. Maurice said in a straightforward manner.

I felt like James Bond. I took the bag and put it on my lap when a middle-aged businesswoman came over and greeted Dr. Maurice. We both stood. Dr. Maurice told her I was a college student researching Red Cross doctors who had been on missions to developing nations. I nodded in accord. I thanked Dr. Maurice, got up, and paid the $70 bill with my credit card, realizing it was how much I had lived on during the past week of camping. But I couldn't complain as Dr. Maurice had just provided me with invaluable information.

After a few days on the road, I called Dr. Giles. To my immediate surprise, we were only a half hour away from his home in the French countryside. He was there vacationing with his family. We met on the main road and followed him up the hill to his country home in our rental car. I sat in his office, and he talked about working with the Red Cross and about the prisoners' conditions. He was as jovial as Azeddine had described. After our lengthy discussion, he showed me around his home.

When Terry returned from a walk, we thanked Dr. Giles and his family for their hospitality, leaving to look for a place to set up camp. Our luck ran out the next morning when I ran over a rock in the road and broke the gas line on the car. We weren't too far from Dr. Giles's, so I headed back to his place, knocked on the door, and told him what had happened.

While we waited for the car rental agency to bring us another car and tow away the damaged one, Dr. Giles invited us to have lunch with him and his family. We sat outside in the garden and had a wonderful French lunch of bread, cheese, salad, fish; all served with a splash of various wines. The car arrived so we thanked Dr. Giles and company for their generosity once again. After getting another rental car, we headed to the land of Human Rights and the International Court of Justice—Switzerland.

Muslims believe for the most part that life is predestined; God has a plan for us all. Azeddine accepted the fact that the years he'd spent as a prisoner were part of Allah's greater scheme, but so many issues were still unresolved in his mind. He remained steadfast. There had to be some purpose behind why certain things happened in the world. Allah would one day reveal his reasons but, for now, Azeddine would have to live on in hope of future wisdom.

Azeddine watched the sun's rays fade behind the camp. He thought about his home and family. He also wondered what the Polisario's fate would be. It had been twenty years now, and they weren't exactly thriving. The halcyon days had ended long ago, and their dissolution was imminent. How much longer could Algeria support their cause? They hadn't received a new truck, let alone a visit from an Algerian delegate, in over three years. All of these details were disclosed to the United Nation's High Commission for Refugees (UNHCR) after a group of UN investigators visited the camps. Azeddine gave any organizations that came to the camps all the information he could.

"So, what you're saying, Dr. Benmansour, is that the refugee children are being shipped away to Cuba?" probed the young lady who was working with a French foundation. She must have been of North African descent because she spoke a dialect similar to Darija.

"That's right," Azeddine said. He was sitting across from her in the infirmary, now full of supplies Dr. Maurice and Dr. Giles had donated on behalf of the Red Cross. "Many of the Saharawi children are taken away from their families and shipped there."

"Doctor, how is Cuba involved here?"

"How do I know?" He thought and then added, "Cuban doctors come here, as do other Cuban delegates. Children are taken and sent off all the time. I don't know how or why." He was able to talk openly as their interviews were conducted in the absence of guards. The Polisario did this so the visitors would feel they had nothing to hide. Their tricks still worked with the UN, one of the last organizations who hadn't caught on to the Polisario's deceptive tactics.

"Doctor, thank you. I have a couple more questions. This will be a lot easier if you just answer truthfully."

"What I've been telling you is the truth."

"Let me ask," she continued, beads of sweat glistened on her forehead, "have you ever witnessed arms deals or the selling of merchandise that would perhaps seem illegal?"

"Everything they do here is illegal. Every minute we prisoners are here is illegal. They sell our food to Mauritania. They trade arms. They confiscate our packages. They even force you visitors to buy the camels you use while you're here, at three times the cost, then they keep them when you leave."

The young lady had a disconcerted look on her face.

"Organizations giving money to terrorists!" Azeddine said ardently.

Looking back, Azeddine wished the interview had gone more smoothly, but his candor had paid off. After going to the camps to interview prisoners and seeing their condition, these organizations soon shifted sides and began fighting for their release. Maybe this was the catalyst needed for the Polisario's demise.

After they left, the camp was back to normal. Another year came and went. Azeddine thought he would probably never return to Morocco or see his family again. He was almost fifty, and he was reconciled with the idea of dying far from home, buried beneath the sands in a land that once had blossomed.

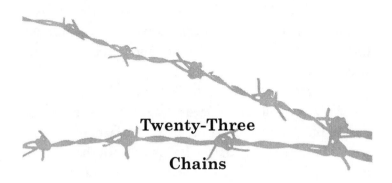

Twenty-Three

Chains

Late 2003

THE DAY came as a blur in the Douze Octobre. Azeddine was signing a medical document for a prisoner who needed to be taken to Rabonée for treatment. He stopped writing midway and stared at the date. It had now been twenty-four years to the day in August since the bloody massacre in Lebouirate. Twenty-four years since his capture. It was another year, another despondent anniversary.

With the help of the Red Cross and other NGOs, many of the camps had gotten additional water cisterns and supplies to build proper housing. When the aiding organizations finally realized the Polisario was stealing funds, they laid down new regulations to ensure the prisoners benefited from the money and supplies donated. The new system of checks and balances worked on the principal that if the NGOs saw evident improvements, then money would keep filtering in.

Azeddine noticed he had written the year 1979 instead of 2003. Over the last several months, he was making little mistakes like this. Usually sharp-minded, the stress and years were taking their toll on his mind and body. He decided to rest for the night.

Lahassan's son entered the infirmary the next morning. He was a Polisario guard rising to higher positions due to his dead father's influence. His father had died where he wanted, in battle. Lahassan's son had grown up around the camps and knew many of the prisoners by name. Azeddine noticed he looked a lot like Lahassan in the eyes, but he could see a spark of compassion his father had never possessed. The son had been to both Spain and Cuba to study.

"Dr. Azeddine."

Azeddine kept writing. He couldn't hear the young guard who approached his right ear.

"Dr. Azeddine," he said once again, tapping on the desk.

"Yes, yes. What do you need?"

"Are you keeping track of everything for the Red Cross?"

"Yes, they have asked me to do so. The Head of Security reviews it all each week as well." Azeddine looked over the top of the glasses that Dr. Maurice had personally sent him.

"Is your registration number with them, your E.H.T., 00612?"

"I have no idea what that number means, but yes, that is my *number*.

"You are to report with your baggage for transport. Tomorrow, nine a.m."

Over the last several years, Azeddine had taken a few minutes between patients or before roll call to pray. But now, at his older age, he took his time to say all five prayers, not caring if the guards told him to hurry. Those five times a day, for him, were meant to be dedicated to Allah, a time to think about his father in God's care. He no longer cared about the threats of punishment, the beatings.

As he pronounced the prayers, repeated Allah's names, and prostrated to the eastern horizon, he imagined his father watching him. He pictured his father's face as he held the prayer beads his mother had sent him.

The dreams of his house with the mantel and blowing curtains had subsided some years ago. He had new dreams, ones that were surreal images of a world like the desert, but where the Earth, Allah, and man were closer, somehow. His inner thoughts and deepest feelings surfaced when he prayed. He didn't want to let go of that—the only connection he had to his father's memory.

"Move to the trucks. We're taking you to Rabonée."

"Rabonée?"

Each prisoner had to go through a physical examination and was told to keep quiet throughout the day. Another influx of prisoners soon arrived to undergo the same procedure.

Azeddine looked closely for Ahmed, who had been moved to Camp Dahkla, but didn't see him. Following the examinations, they were taken to a building with interior décor that would impress even a king. Sitting against the wall, prisoners were called one by one. Azeddine was fingerprinted and asked questions regarding his age, rank, and birthday. By evening, he and the other fifty prisoners had been inspected and taken to barracks he had never seen.

For the next four days, Azeddine waited to find out why this strange procedure was taking place. On the fifth day, he saw a white Land Rover drive into the camp. The doctor who descended from the vehicle was wearing an emblem he knew all too well.

The news that day, September 1, 2003, flooded the camp in a matter of seconds, washing over everyone as a cleansing wave, quenching a thirst that only those held deep in the Sahara could truly feel.

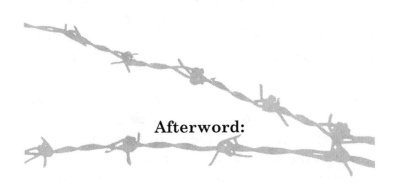

Afterword:

Some prisoners were set free before Dr. Azeddine Benmansour. He was one of many released that day, but over a thousand remained. He had been officially held as a POW for twenty-four years and seven days in Polisario camps, one of the longest POW detentions in world history.

After being flown with Red Cross delegates to Agadir, Azeddine was taken home to Fez, where he was reunited with his mother and other family members. He has recently started practicing medicine again, wishing to keep busy as he reacquaints himself with modern Morocco. He is learning how to drive again and catching up on all the latest scientific and technological advances. He even has a cell phone.

Within a short time, Azeddine has been blessed with a family of his own. His eloquent wife is from Rabat; the two met through family friends. In their marriage ceremony, caught on videotape, the two happily sit close together in customary wedding clothes, with traditional music and foods. That moment was a dream long awaited. Azeddine now sits peacefully with his toddler boy on his knee, his wife tending to the new baby girl.

Dr. Ahmed, Azeddine's friend and companion throughout the story, resides in Fez. The two get together as often as possible, sharing stories of their new lives spent around those they love.

Azeddine and the author still communicate regularly. The two recently shared a Ramadan meal prepared with care by Azeddine's wife. They watched videos of his marriage and of his son as an infant. Azeddine still dreams of his father. One vision he often has is of his father approaching; without talking, he reminds Azeddine that faith and love, no matter how much time passes, triumph over all.

Author's Acknowledgements

I would like to thank the International Red Cross/Crescent (IRC) and their staff, faculty, and doctors. Also, I have to mention those organizations and people in France and elsewhere: Amnesty International; Human Rights Watch; Afifa Karmouss with France Libertés; Madame Dominque Rambaud who works with the European Parliament and oversees the Maghreb area, aiding in the coordination of Liberty Passports; Association of Victims of Human Rights Violations in Polisario Prisons (ASVIPO). In Morocco, I'd like to extend a gracious thank you to Azeddine, his mother, and other family members who treated me as their own; Amine Filali, who helped me get started, and his father and family, all who introduced Azeddine and his story to me; working for MINURSO in Layoune, I'd like to give special thanks to Rachid and other Moroccans working in Western Sahara; Al Akhawayn University in Ifrane; Peace Corps Morocco; and the Friends of Morocco.

In the United States, I'd like to give a special thanks to Sandy Tritt at *tritt.wirefire.com* for her creative talents; the West Virginia Writers, Inc.; the James Jones Literary Society; Sherice at iElectrify.com for her wonderful design expertise; the editor(s) of *Combat Magazine* who first published some excerpts from this book; Dr. William Zartman with Johns Hopkins University; Andrew Sinclair and David H. Cowan for their historical and political analysis; author Erich Krauss for showing me the ropes; Ariele Huff for her amazing eye for editing; Susan Reed for brilliant typesetting and superb Morocco map; Shaun Kilgore for our writing talks; Brent Pasley and Derek Keele for their support, along with Ramiza Koya, Emily Gill, Katie Dutcher, and Brooke Mackenzie. I'd like to especially express my gratitude to author Ray Elliott and his wife Vanessa Faurie. Finally, I owe my world to Fazia Farrook, who offered unyielding support, patience, and inspiration; my mother and step-father Carlos; my father, David; and my twin brother, Terry Hollowell, who flew to the desert and beyond with me while researching this material.